VOICES FROM THE MARGINS

VOICES FROM THE MARGINS

An Annotated Bibliography of
Fiction on Disabilities and
Differences for Young People

MARILYN WARD

Library of Congress Cataloging-in-Publication Data

Ward, Marilyn.
    Voices from the margins : an annotated bibliography of fiction on disabilities and differences for young people / Marilyn Ward.
        p.   cm.
    Includes indexes.
    ISBN 978-1-59311-400-8 (alk.   paper)
        1. Young adult fiction, American—Bibliography.   2. People with disabilities in literature—Bibliography.   3. Difference (Psychology) in literature—Bibliography.
    4. Marginality, Social, in literature—Bibliography.   I. Title.
    Z1231.F4.W36   2002
    [PS648.Y68]
    016.813008′03520816—dc21   2002276832

British Library Cataloguing in Publication Data is available.

Library of Congress Catalog Card Number: 2002276832
ISBN: 0–313–31798–4

First published in 2002

Printed in the United States of America

The paper used in this book complies with the
Permanent Paper Standard issued by the National
Information Standards Organization (Z39.48–1984).

10 9 8 7 6 5 4 3 2 1

For my father

Thanks to Rhonda Branch, Amy Holm, June Ward, and Tui Wyllie
for their valuable assistance

Thanks to Lynn Malloy, my editor, for her expertise and vision

Contents

Introduction

I have entered high school with the wrong hair, the wrong clothes, the wrong attitude. And I don't have anyone to sit with.

—Melinda, high school freshman
Speak by Laurie Halse Anderson

I'm wired bad, or wired mad, or wired sad, or wired glad. But there is no doubt about it, I'm wired.

—Joey, middle-grader
Joey Pigza Swallowed the Key by Jack Gantos

Welcome to Wheelchair World.

—David, eighth grader
Rebound by Eric Walters

Talk to me, not about me.

—Sarah, twelve-year-old
On Being Sarah by Elizabeth Helfman

These are the voices of young people who have been marginalized by their obvious and not-so-obvious disabilities and differences. They are puzzle pieces that don't fit in, square pegs, kids who are picked last for teams, and children who sit alone in the lunchroom. They are called hurtful names. They're treated as if they don't exist. They desperately want to fit in and have friends, but they usually fail to do so. *Voices from the Margins* is for and about readers like Melinda, Joey, David, and Sarah and their teachers, librarians, families, and friends. It is for everyone who is personally and professionally involved with young people and books and for everyone who wants to listen to voices from the margins.

Since the passage of Public Law 94–142, the Education for All Handicapped Children Act, in 1975, all children have been guaranteed an equal education in the "least restrictive environment." This has prompted mainstreaming and inclusion programs for millions of special education students, whereby these students have been placed in regular education classrooms for all or most of the school day. Consequently, teachers have had to adjust their teaching methods and materials to accommodate all students. Mainstreaming, inclusion, individualized education plans, computers, Braille typewriters, and audiotaped books are among the tools used.

An often overlooked tool, which is common and relatively inexpensive, is literature. Indeed, literature about disabilities and differences can affect the reader's attitudes and feelings and can increase one's awareness of and sensitivity to those disabilities and differences. For young people who are not disabled, who may not know a person with a disability or difference, and who seem to "fit in," their only exposure to the disability or difference might be through books. For young people with disabilities or differences, characters in books they read influence how they view themselves. Therefore, literature about disabilities and differences can be a powerful tool to heighten the achievement of all students by broadening their attitudes and perceptions of self and others.

Voices from the Margins: An Annotated Bibliography of Fiction on Disabilities and Differences for Young People is a bibliography to help teachers, librarians, special education professionals, reading resource staff, school administrators, healthcare practitioners, and parents select and use children's and young adult fiction that features characters with disabilities and differences. It is a unique and much needed collection development tool for school and public libraries. And for young readers looking for good reads featuring characters with disabilities or differences, *Voices from the Margins* may spark a healthy acceptance of self and others. It is my hope that those personally and professionally involved with young people and books will find this annotated bibliography valuable and easy to use.

Titles were located by contacting publishers of children's and young adult literature, conducting computer searches, and browsing through bookstores and libraries. The literature gleaned for this bibliography was published between 1990 and 2001 and includes picture books, middle-grade chapter books, and young adult novels. The majority of the titles have been published since 1998. Most are in print. Out-of-print books are identified in the annotations. Out-of-print books can be located through Amazon.com Marketplace, Advanced Book Exchange, Inc. (abebooks.com), and various other out-of-print book services. Out-of-print books can also be found in school and public library collections, where they can continue to affect readers for many years.

The Hedberg Library at Carthage College, Kenosha, Wisconsin, has collected the books cited in this reference work. Through OCLC, an international database, to which the Hedberg Library belongs, the collection is available for interlibrary loan.

HOW TO USE THIS BOOK

Voices from the Margins can be used to obtain information about children's and young adult fiction in two ways: to learn the titles, authors, and age levels of books on a particular subject, such as "cerebral palsy" or "dyslexia"; or to ascertain the subject (or subjects) when only the title, or author and title, are known. For example, if the title *Speak* is known, this volume will enable the user to discover that *Speak* was written by Laurie Halse Anderson and published by Farrar, Straus & Giroux in 1999, and that it concerns the subjects "elective mutism," "emotional problems," and "high school."

For ease and convenience of use, *Voices from the Margins* is divided into five sections:

Annotated Bibliography

Title Index

Author Index

Age-level Index

Subject Index

Annotated Bibliography

This section is arranged alphabetically by author. Each entry is numbered and is listed with complete bibliographic information in this order: author, title, publisher, date of publication, hardcover or paperback edition, number of pages, suggested age level, International Standard Book Number (ISBN), price, illustrator, and subject headings.

115 McElfresh, Lynn E. *Can You Feel the Thunder?* Simon & Schuster. 1999. Hardcover 144pp. Ages: 12 and up. ISBN: 0–689–82324–X $16.00. Subjects: baseball, blind, deaf, dyscalculia, learning disabled, middle school, physically handicapped, siblings, sports

Each entry also includes a brief plot summary, some critical comments, and relevant notes (author credentials, appendixes, etc.) Artistic medium and style in picture books are addressed. Quotations are sometimes included to serve as examples of the author's skill or to show how a character is portrayed. The length of an entry does not indicate a book's quality or importance, because some plots can be summarized more concisely than others.

Title Index

This section contains an alphabetical list of all titles in the bibliography with authors' names in parentheses, followed by the entry number of the full listing in the Annotated Bibliography.

Petey (Mikaelsen, Ben), 120

Author Index

This section contains an alphabetical list of all authors whose works are included in the Annotated Bibliography. Each author's name is followed by the book title and the entry number of the full listing.

Howe, James, *The Misfits*, 80

Age-level Index

This section lists all books by age level as suggested by publishers and reviewers. Some books may be appropriate for younger or older audiences, depending on a student's reading ability and maturity, whether the book will be used for a unit or for independent reading, and the skill and enthusiasm of the adults working with the young readers.

Subject Index

This subject index to two hundred books for children and young adults is catalogued under nearly ninety subject headings, which are arranged alphabetically. Subject headings reflect established terms commonly used in school and public libraries, for example, "blind," "learning disabled," and general subjects as "music," "nature," and "sports." This index provides a means of identifying all those books that may contain information or material on a particular subject. If, for example, the user wants books with characters who are deaf, the Subject Index reveals that under "deaf" there are twenty-six titles with such characters, listed alphabetically by author. Many books concern multiple subjects and are, therefore, listed under all appropriate subject headings. For example, *Moses Goes to a Concert* by Isaac Millman can be found under the subject headings "deaf," "elementary school," "music," "physically handicapped," "sign language," and "special education."

A note on the "elementary school," "middle school," and "high school" subject headings: they refer to grades K–5, 6–8, and 9–12, respectively. They indicate schools attended by characters where classroom settings are essential to the story. They do not necessarily reflect suggested audience age levels.

THE BOOKS

Picture books, contemporary realistic fiction, historical fiction, mysteries, fantasies, and poetry are all included in this reference work.

Picture Books

Picture books convey meaning in both the artwork and the text. Family stories, everyday experiences, cultural diversity, the natural world, humor, fantasy, and social and environmental concerns are presented in picture books. These books also portray the experiences of people with disabilities and differences. An important recent development in picture books is that more and more books are geared to children in middle grades and to young adults. Some of the picture books included in this bibliography are designed for very young children, for example, *Susan Laughs* by Jeanne Willis and *It's Okay to be Different* by Todd Parr. In others, the sophisticated subjects and richly detailed illustrations are ideal to enhance the education of middle graders and young adults. In order for these books to be utilized to their full extent, they need to be promoted through booktalks, reading lists, and book displays. Examples of picture books suitable for older readers are *Seal Surfer* by Michael Foreman, *The Hickory Chair* by Lisa Rowe Fraustino, and *Arabella* by Wendy Orr.

Contemporary Realistic Fiction

Contemporary realistic fiction honestly portrays the realities of life and helps children and young adults gain a fuller understanding of the problems and issues of living today. Many of the stories in this bibliography are about growing up and finding a place in the family, among peers, and in our modern society. In addition, aspects of coping with disabilities and differences may be found in this type of literature. Contemporary realistic fiction helps young people enlarge their frames of reference while seeing the world from another perspective. In *Rebound* by Eric Walters, seventh-grader Sean learns about David's wheelchair world when he uses David's spare wheelchair and accompanies him through town. Contemporary realistic fiction can illuminate other experiences that young people have not had. A child who takes school for granted might gain much from Brian, in *My Name Is ~~Brain~~ Brian* by Jeanne Betancourt. Brian is dyslexic and desperately wants to succeed in school. School stories offer children and young adults the comfort of the familiar. Students recognize settings with lockers and lunchrooms; characters like the friendly principal, the class bully, and the understanding teacher or coach; and situations such as the science fair, spring musical, school dance, or championship game. All the disabilities and differences addressed in *Voices from the Margins* are represented in school stories. Simple school stories with important themes for beginning readers and middle graders are *Lucy's Picture* by Nicola Moon and *Marrying Malcolm Murgatroyd* by Mame Farrell. Thought-provoking school stories for older readers are *Teacher's Pet* by Laurie Halse Anderson and *Whale Talk* by Chris Crutcher.

Contemporary realistic fiction also reassures young people that they are not the first in the world to have faced their problems. In Sharon Flakes's *The Skin I'm In*, seventh-grader Maleeka believes that she is a freak because she is too dark, too tall, and too skinny. With the help of her teacher, whose face is blotched with a giant white mark, Maleeka discovers that she is not alone and learns an important lesson about acceptance. And in Eve Eliot's *Insatiable: The Compelling Story of Four Teens, Food, and Its Power*, Samantha, Hannah, Phoebe, and Jessica, whose self-perceptions lead to eating disorders, realize that they have similar problems and can learn from each other.

In many works of contemporary realistic fiction, the feelings of siblings are examined with compassion. In *Ian's Walk: A Story about Autism* by Laurie Lears, Julie feels her own life is swallowed up by the attention focused on her brother Ian and his autism. Her frustration and anger are obvious, yet when Ian gets lost, she finds herself caring for him and loving him. Likewise, in *Can You Feel the Thunder?* by Lynn E. McElfresh, seventh-grader Mic is embarrassed by his older sister Stephanie, who is deaf and blind. He comes to terms with his feelings about her disabilities and appreciates her special understanding of him.

Many contemporary realistic fiction books paint positive pictures of people with disabilities or differences. *Don't Call Me Marda* by Sheila Kelly

Welch describes eleven-year-old Marsha and her family's decision to adopt eight-year-old developmentally delayed Wendy. And *Of Sound Mind* by Jean Ferris depicts a high school boy who is the only one in his family who can hear. Both of these books and the others in this annotated bibliography show how families deal courageously with disabilities and differences.

Through contemporary realistic fiction, readers can develop a more intelligent understanding of some of the challenges faced by persons who are on the margins because of their disabilities and differences.

Historical Fiction

Voices from the margins are also apparent in historical fiction. Increased use of books across the curriculum has created a demand for this type of literature. Exciting, well-written historical fiction captures the interest of young readers and helps them experience the past. Through these books, children and young adults can enter into the conflicts, the sufferings, and the joys of those who lived before, and learn to appreciate that disabilities and differences are not just contemporary concerns.

Many young readers are intrigued with ancient times and tales. *The Raging Quiet* by Sherryl Jordan, which is set in an ancient time and place, concerns disabilities and differences. Raven is deaf, and Marnie is accused of witchcraft. The story, with its lively plot, provides an enthralling look at women's roles, how a deaf young man is misunderstood and mistreated, and the justice of the time. The text and illustrations of *Silent Lotus* by Jeanne Lee present a charming view of life in ancient Cambodia. Lotus, who cannot hear or speak, grows from a lonely and unhappy girl to the most famous dancer in the Khmer kingdom.

Students are often interested in fiction about the American frontier, the Civil War, and World Wars I and II. One story of the American frontier is *Prairie School* by Avi. Here, Aunt Dora, who uses a wheelchair, enlightens readers about the flora and fauna of the prairie and the joy of books. In another frontier story, *Through the Open Door* by Joy N. Hulme, a nine-year-old girl, who cannot speak, gives a compelling account of pioneer life and her own struggle with her speech disorder.

A work of historical fiction set after the Civil War is *Mary Mehan Awake* by Jennifer Armstrong. This book takes a look at young Irish immigrant Mary, her relationship with a man who became deaf during the Civil War, and her recovery from the pain, sorrow, and suffering she witnessed during the war. World War I is the setting for *Charlie Wilcox* by Sharon McKay. In this powerful adventure novel, a physically disabled fourteen-year-old boy leaves his native Newfoundland to work in a mobile hospital unit in France.

All the Way Home by Patricia Reilly Giff takes place during World War II. It paints a portrait of life on the homefront, including a girl with polio, the Brooklyn Dodgers, and President Franklin Roosevelt.

Historical fiction about life in countries other than the United States promotes students' geographic literacy, spatial perception, and global awareness. It also demonstrates that disabilities and differences occur worldwide. *The Storyteller's Beads* by Jane Kurtz offers a glimpse of life in Ethiopia, as told by Rahel, who is blind. And in *Mind's Eye* by Paul Fleischman, although set in contemporary North Dakota, sixteen-year-old Courtney, who cannot walk, and eighty-eight-year-old Elva transport readers to 1910 Italy.

In addition to presenting another time and place, fictional books set in the past invite a comparison with the present. *Petey* by Ben Mikaelsen is the life story of a person with cerebral palsy. It also chronicles the history of how people with disabilities have been treated in this country over the last seventy-five years. Petey's early experiences are unimaginable by today's standards.

Opportunities for critical thinking and judgment are built into historical novels that set forth conflicting views on an issue and force characters to make difficult choices. Readers of *Water at the Blue Earth* by Ann Howard Creel will struggle as twelve-year-old Wren did with her crucial decision to warn the blind Indian's people of an upcoming attack.

Historical fiction can help readers see that times change but universal needs do not. All people, including those who have disabilities and differences, need and want respect, belonging, and freedom, whether they lived during ancient times, the American frontier, the Civil War, the World Wars, or are alive today.

Mysteries

In addition, mysteries are included in this annotated bibliography. Children and young adults are proud to match wits with clever young sleuths and solve mysteries. As in the real world, both detectives and victims have disabilities and differences. *Hasta Luego, San Diego* by Jean Andrews finds the Flying Fingers Club using sign language and their detective skills to solve the mystery of the missing San Diego Zoo cockatoos. *Checkers* by John Marsden is a suspense story set in Australia about a fifteen-year-old girl who recounts through group therapy her mental breakdown, the collapse of her family, and the mystery surrounding her father's corrupt business deal. Readers never discover what happened to outcast Chris Creed in *The Body of Christopher Creed* by Carol Plum-Ucci.

The story offers plot twists and an eye-opening look at alienation, and it stresses compassion toward those who are different. These books are examples of mysteries that combine characters who are disabled or different with cliffhanger action, terror, romance, and vivid human emotions.

Fantasy

Voices from children and young adults on the margins can be heard in works of fantasy, as well. This genre is of value for children and young adults because it reveals new insights into the world of reality and helps readers develop their imaginations. In *Gathering Blue* by Lois Lowry, Kira, who is physically disabled, is amazed to discover her talents and is awestruck and apprehensive in the face of the different tasks she must undertake. *Gathering Blue* also raises questions about the organization of society and the nature of a future world.

Poetry

Poetry is also included in this bibliography and can express the same content as realistic fiction. Poetry is the distillation of experience that captures the essence of an object, a feeling, or a thought. Because each word must be chosen carefully for both sound and meaning, poetry says what it says very intensely. The poetry included in this bibliography reflects the challenges of growing up in America and powerfully deals with disabilities, differences, and the feelings of troubled young people. For example, selections in *The Other Me: Poetic Thoughts on ADD for Adults, Kids, and Parents* by Wilma Fellman describes the mixed feelings of pride and despair felt by a child who has attention-deficit disorder. And Mattie J. T. Stepanek, an eleven-year-old boy with muscular dystrophy, writes about loneliness, fear, and hope in his poems in *Journey through Heartsongs*. Poetry can speak to the needs and interests of children and young adults with and without disabilities or differences. For all children and young adults, it not only mirrors life, but it reveals life in new dimensions.

The world of children's and young adult literature is broad indeed. Young readers can become deeply engrossed in what they read. It is, therefore, of prime importance to use this powerful literature to affect young readers' attitudes and feelings and to increase their sensitivity to disabilities and differences.

SELECTION OF BOOKS

Selection of books in this bibliography has been guided by the six criteria that follow. The annotations are from one perspective. I did not include titles I would not recommend personally.

Criteria for Selection of Books

1. Accuracy of Information

Accurate information must be presented in the book, including the use of current technology to describe the disability or difference, medical treatments, rehabilitation measures, and socialization issues.

2. Literary Quality

The book must be well written in a clear style. Standards ought to be just as rigorous when considering literature about disabilities and differences as they would be when choosing any other children's or young adult book.

3. Realistic and Believable Portrayal of People

Negative and false stereotypes about people with disabilities or differences should be avoided. Characters in books should not be portrayed as victims or heroes but instead as being capable of fully participating in everyday life such as making friends, attending school, dating, and having relationships with parents and siblings. Characters with disabilities or differences should be multidimensional, rounded, and complex; their prominent traits should focus on what they can do, as opposed to what they cannot do. Books should point out that characters with disabilities or differences have the same kinds of experiences, dreams, successes, and failures that other readers do.

4. Settings That Are Integral to the Action and Characters

The characters with disabilities or differences should be presented in a realistic setting. This includes descriptions of modifications to home environments and school situations. With the current emphasis on placement in general education classrooms, if special classes or schools are depicted in a book, it should be made clear that there are good reasons for removing the students from the mainstream and placing them in specially designed classrooms.

5. Reasonable Story Resolution

The story resolution should be believable and reasonable. Characters should learn to accept their disabilities or differences and focus their efforts on their abilities, or just learn how to live with and in spite of their disabilities or differences. Fairytale endings or oversimplified cures are not believable and are not solutions for the conflicts or problems of people with disabilities or differences.

    6.   Audience: Age-level and Genre

This collection is focused on fiction books that would be of interest to elementary through high school readers. Designation of age level is based on suggestions by publishers and reviewers. Such suggestions are subjective; users of this reference work will want to apply their own evaluations.

An Annotated Bibliography of Fiction on Disabilities and Differences for Young People

1 Abbott, Deborah, and Henry Kisor. *One TV Blasting and a Pig Outdoors.* Albert Whitman and Co. 1994. Hardcover 40pp. Ages: 9–12. ISBN: 0–8075–6075–8 $14.95. Illustrated by Leslie Morrill.

Middle-schooler Conan starts his story by describing his world, which is full of sound, noise, and chatter. His dad's world is very different. His dad is deaf. Meningitis destroyed his hearing when he was three years old. Conan tells what it's like to have a deaf father. His father lip-reads. It's not easy because so many sounds look alike. He sometimes makes funny mistakes. When Conan's little brother once asked, "What's that big noise?" his dad replied with a puzzled look, "What pig outdoors?" Conan's dad doesn't know sign language. As a boy there weren't other deaf children in his town, so he took speech lessons. Conan explains that some deaf people learn sign language first and then learn to speak. Conan's dad is glad he learned speech and lip-reading. Conan discusses labels, like profoundly deaf, hearing-impaired, the deaf culture, and hard-of-hearing. He also informs readers about technological advances, like vibrating pagers, TTY (teletypewriters), closed captioned televisions, and cochlear implants, which make the lives of deaf people much easier. Conan tells his friends who are nervous about talking to his dad to talk to him as they would to anyone else's father: Speak distinctly, listen carefully, and make sure Dad is looking. Nine full-page watercolors are interspersed throughout this humorous and informative account of a boy and his dad who view deafness not as a handicap but as a challenge. A thorough two-page glossary is included.

Subjects: deaf, middle school, physically handicapped

2 Anderson, Laurie Halse. *Speak.* Farrar, Straus & Giroux. 1999. Hardcover 198pp. Ages: 12 and up. ISBN: 0–374–37152–0 $16.00.

Ninth-grader Melinda Sordino called 911 from an end-of-summer teen drinking party. Because of this, her friends stop talking to her. People she doesn't even know harass her and hate her. But the memory of the party stays, and the guilt and anger eat away at her. She hardly speaks at all. It's easier to not say anything. Her grades plummet. She is a social outcast. Melinda is "seriously weird in the head" because she was raped by popular senior Andy "Beast" Evans at that late-summer party, and she can't tell anyone. But when Melinda's former best friend, Rachel, starts dating the Beast, Melinda knows she has to do something. In a note to Rachel, she reveals why she called the police. It was not to break up the party. It was because of the sexual assault. And in a painful confrontation with Andy, she finds her voice, screams, and "no!" explodes from her. Now she will be able to speak the truth. The first-person narrative of an isolated teenager made silent by a tragic incident, presented in the context of an insightful look at contemporary high school life, will engage readers.

Subjects: elective mutism, emotional problems, high school

3   Anderson, Laurie Halse. *Teacher's Pet* (Wild At Heart Series #7). Pleasant Co. 2001. Paperback 136pp. Ages: 12 and up. ISBN: 1–58485–055–8 $4.95.

Number 7 in the Wild at Heart series, a spin-off of the American Girl stories, features seventh-grader Maggie MacKenzie, who has been living with her grandmother since her parents were killed in a car accident. Gran is a feisty veterinarian who owns the Wild at Heart Animal Clinic, where Maggie does volunteer work. Maggie is unhappy about starting middle school until she meets her biology teacher, Mr. Carlson, and his guide dog, Scout. Maggie is confused and wonders how a teacher can be blind. Mr. Carlson explains that two years ago retinitis pigmentosa made him blind. He took time off from teaching, went to a special school, learned to read Braille, and got Scout. He stresses that Scout is a working dog and must not be bothered so he can stay focused on his job. He also describes guide dog puppy-raising and the five months of training school necessary to graduate successful guide dogs. Maggie, who has a gift for working with animals, notices that Mr. Carlson and Scout haven't formed the bond of trust they need to be a real team. She offers tips to Mr. Carlson and encourages him, and slowly the blind teacher and his guide dog make progress. But then, an accident occurs that sends Scout to the clinic for emergency surgery. Here, Mr. Carlson realizes how much Scout means to him. Scout is not his tool. He's his companion. And Scout hears Mr. Carlson's voice and decides to fight for his life. Scout will recover, and after some retraining Scout and Mr. Carlson will be a confident, comfortable team for a long time. Maggie's first-person narrative describes veterinary procedures in easy language and builds suspense in this likable and informative story about a working guide dog team. The book concludes with more information about guide dogs and a questionnaire, "Do You Have Puppy Raising Potential?"

Subjects: blind, dogs—service, grandparents, intergenerational relationships, middle school, physically handicapped, service dogs, teachers

4   Anderson, Marcella Fisher. *Reflections from a Mud Puddle: Helping Children Cope and Grow*. Boyds Mills Press. 1998. Paperback 96pp. Ages: 9–12. ISBN: 1–56397–606–4 $14.95. Illustrated by Christopher Wray.

This collection of short stories from "Highlights for Children" and topic-related poetry helps children deal with the challenges in their lives and helps adults when working with such children. Ten topics, ranging from "Changes in the Family" to "Tomorrow Will Be Better," organize the materials that were compiled by an authority on bibliotherapy, the use of literature to help children and young adults confront the challenges in their own lives. In "Gabe the Great," an overweight boy lacks self-esteem and is teased by his soccer teammates. He wins the game and learns that the size of his heart matters more than the size of his body. "Joey and the Fourth-of-July Duck" tells of lonely Joey, who is developmentally delayed. Wearing glasses is a problem for Becky and Jake in "Eye Trouble or a Close Encounter of a Nutty Kind." Meg in "Riding the Wind" uses a wheelchair but can handle a sailboat anyway. Hearing-impaired Marie, in "Thorgersturm: Voice in the Storm," uses her lip-reading skills to save her schoolmates during an autumn storm. And in "The Homecoming," Vanessa worries about seeing her best friend, Mary Margaret, whose face was burned in an accident. Selections also address emotional challenges, friendship, loss, hospital experiences, shyness, siblings, and more. Eileen Spinelli, Lee Bennett Hopkins, Jack Prelutsky, and Jane Yolen are among the well-known authors who are represented in the anthology. Each section suggests a related picture book and offers discussion questions. A thorough subject index improves access to the materials that all relate to challenges confronting children and young adults.

Subjects: burn injuries, elementary school, facial disfiguration, mentally handicapped, middle school, overweight, physically handicapped, poetry, self-perception, short stories, siblings, spina bifida, sports, visually handicapped, wheelchairs

5   Andrews, Jean F. *Hasta Luego, San Diego* (Flying Fingers Series). Kendall Green Publications (Gallaudet University Press). 1991. Paperback 94pp. Ages: 9–12. ISBN: 0-930323-83-1 $4.95.

The third Flying Fingers Club book finds learning disabled ten-year-old Donald Dunbar, his eleven-year-old sister, Susan, and their deaf friend, Matt, on a trip from their home in Richmond, Kentucky, to San Diego with Mrs. Dunbar to celebrate Donald's birthday. Mrs. Dunbar is attending a conference, and the kids are looking forward to visiting the San Diego Zoo and hoping for a mystery to solve. They all know sign language and can talk easily by using their hands. At the hotel they meet thirteen-year-old Hector, who they suspect is a victim of abuse. At the zoo the boys witness the theft of rare gang-gang cockatoos. The sleuths discover that Hector is involved in the crime because his father is one of the robbers. The boys are kidnapped by the crooks and left stranded in Mexico. They meet some Mexican teens, one of whom knows how to sign. The teens help rescue the boys and break an illegal gambling casino in Acapulco. Meanwhile, Susan is busy back in San Diego, helping Hector and his mother file a child abuse case against Hector's father and seeing that they receive help from the Children's Protection Agency. The cockatoos are returned to the zoo, and the adventure ends with the Flying Fingers Club eagerly awaiting their next mystery to solve. This action tale for middle readers shows some of the challenges that learning disabled and deaf youngsters face and also some differences between American and Mexican cultures. Chapter titles include diagrams of hand signs for chapter numbers.

Subjects: abuse, birds, deaf, learning disabled, Mexico, mystery, physically handicapped, sign language

6 Armstrong, Jennifer. *Mary Mehan Awake*. Alfred A. Knopf. 1997. Hardcover 119pp. Ages: 12 and up. ISBN: 0–679–88276–6 $18.00.

This creative book starts with a series of letters that sets readers up for this sequel to *The Dreams of Mairhe Mehan*. After nursing soldiers in the Civil War, young Irish immigrant Mairhe, who now uses the American spelling of her name, is recommended by poet Walt Whitman to be a domestic servant to his wildlife photographer friend, Jasper Dorsett. Mary is tired and emotionally exhausted because of the pain and sorrow she witnessed during the war, but she finds a reawakening of her senses in her new life. Each of the novel's five sections focuses on a different sense and begins with Whitman verses. Mary sees colors and light with a photographer's eye as she helps Dorsett photograph birds. She hears sweet sounds again as she describes them to Henry Till, the Dorsetts' stablehand who used to be a musician but became deaf while fighting in the Civil War. All of Mary's senses are renewed as she falls in love with Henry and awakens to the joy and beauty around her. Picturesque imagery and metaphors are woven smoothly into this tender and poetic young adult novel.

Subjects: birds, deaf, historical fiction, music, physically handicapped

7 Avi. *Prairie School*. Harper Collins. 2001. Hardcover 48pp. Ages: 8–12. ISBN: 0–06–027664–9 $14.95. Illustrated by Bill Farnsworth.

In 1880, nine-year-old Noah Bidson and his family move from their farm in Maine to the new state of Colorado. They work hard, and Noah loves the prairie. When Noah's Aunt Dora arrives to give Noah schooling, Noah resists, saying he doesn't need schooling on the prairie. Dora, who uses a wheelchair because she lost the use of her legs in a buggy accident, sets up school in the sod house. Noah does not want to learn to read, and Dora says he is "as stubborn as a downhill mule on an uphill road." But Dora knows what to do. She wheels herself and her book out onto the prairie. She gets Noah to push her, and she asks him questions about the flowers, the stars, and what they see on the prairie. Noah tells what he knows, but Dora looks in her book and tells Noah even more. Noah is fascinated and decides that if he learns to read books, he can read the prairie. Noah practices and learns to read poetry, stories, history, and the Bible to his family. Dora has to return home, but she has taught Noah that he will be his own best teacher. She tells him that her mind can go farther with books than her body can go with her legs. Noah has both, so he will go twice as far. This "I Can Read Chapter Book" with its quiet, simple text and warm-colored, soft paintings reinforces the message that reading can open worlds.

Subjects: books and reading, Colorado, elementary school, historical fiction, nature, wheelchairs

8   Bacon, Katharine Jay. *Finn*. Simon & Schuster. 1998. Hardcover 171pp. Ages: 10 and up. ISBN: 0–689–82216–2 $16.00.

Fifteen-year-old Finn has built walls for his own protection. Inside, terrifying emotions swirl and storm. He is angry. Outside, a scar runs from his forehead to his cheek, a cast holds his left ankle, and a black glove protects his burned right hand. He is mute. Psychiatrists have told him that to regain his power of speech he must relive each step of the tragic small-plane crash that killed his parents and sister and injured him so badly. He now lives on his grandmother's farm in Vermont, where he renews his friendship with thirteen-year-old Julia, a neighbor, who visits every day to train one of his grandmother's horses. Julia and Finn's sister used to be best friends. Julia hurts, too, but she trusts life. She is thoughtful and patient with Finn's psychological inability to speak. Over the summer they unearth a "rat's nest" of troubles. They discover Toq, half-wolf and half-dog, living in the pinewood on the farm. They rescue it from a trap, and it begins to trust them. Toq is wrongly suspected of ravaging several farms, attacking goats and killing a lamb. Adding to their troubles, Julia and Finn stumble upon the supply drop used by a gang of drug dealers. Finn is tempted by the cocaine they find, but he realizes that using it would not be an easy escape out of himself. He truly does want to live a real life again. Finn's recovery is slow, but he finally regains his voice when Julia is dumped into an abandoned well by an addicted cocaine dealer and Finn rides through a thunderstorm and a fire to save her. Shifting viewpoints increase the tension in this novel about a teen who breaks through the walls he has built and deals with his grief.

Subjects: dogs, elective mutism, grandparents, grief, horses, intergenerational relationships, physically handicapped

9 Barrett, Mary Brigid. *Sing to the Stars*. Little, Brown. 1994. Hardcover 32pp. Ages: 5–8. ISBN: 0–316–08224–4. Out of print. Illustrated by Sandra Speidel.

Mr. Washington, who is blind, recognizes young Ephram's "light step, brush, light step, brush" walk home from his violin lesson. Ephram is amazed that the man can tell he's happy by what Mr. Washington calls the song of life in his walk. Mr. Washington enjoys listening to Ephram play Bach after supper, up on the apartment roof. When he encourages Ephram to play in an open mike benefit concert the next night, Ephram is reluctant but wonders about the man's interesting music. Ephram's grandmother explains that Mr. Washington was trained as a classical pianist and was famous as Flash Fingers Washington, who played hot jazz, cool blues, and old spirituals until he lost his sight in an accident. The next morning Ephram tries to persuade Mr. Washington to play with him at the concert, but Mr. Washington has lost his confidence. Mr. Washington does show up at the concert that hot night, though, and when a brownout causes the lights to go out and the crowd gets restless, it's Mr. Washington who heads onto the stage with Ephram. Together they play the sweet sounds of "Amazing Grace." The music sings to the stars. The muted colors in the impressionistic pastel drawings illuminate this engaging story of encouragement. The language is rich in sound imagery and city beat.

Subjects: blind, grandparents, intergenerational relationships, music, physically handicapped

10 Benjamin, E.M.J. *Takedown*. Banks Channel Books. 1999. Paperback 205pp. Ages: 12 and up. ISBN: 1–889199–04–4 $9.95.

High school senior Jake Chapman is seventh in his class, recipient of a Navy ROTC scholarship, Maynard High's most valuable wrestler, and likely to win the state wrestling championship. But everything is threatened when he starts having seizures and is diagnosed with epilepsy. Because people are afraid of epilepsy and because they think it means he can't do things, Jake becomes "The Great Liar" and doesn't tell anyone about his condition.

He lies to his fellow wrestlers because he's afraid he will be kicked off the team, and he even breaks up with his girlfriend because he can't trust her not to tell. He has to give up driving for a while and learn to be responsible about his medication. But Jake's coach finds out about the epilepsy and reminds Jake of his goal, his talent, and his will to achieve it. And Jake's dad warns him of "cocooning" when Jakes spends all his time lifting weights and running so he won't have to face anyone. Ultimately Jake's discipline and adaptability permit him to successfully reorder his life and reach his goal. Two characters add to this gripping sports story. Chopper is Jake's very likable younger computer-geek brother. And Gary Hanson is a wrestler who is blind and tells Jake that "handicap is a state of mind . . . (it's) relative . . . (and) people need to know." The book delivers accurate information about epilepsy while relating Jake's and his family's adjustment to his experience.

Subjects: blind, epilepsy, high school, seizure disorder, sports, wrestling

11 Betancourt, Jeanne. *My Name Is ~~Brain~~ Brian*. Scholastic. 1993. Paperback 128pp. Ages 9–12. ISBN: 0–590–44922–2 $4.50.

Brian hates the thought of starting sixth grade because school is so difficult for him. His parents just think he's lazy. He really hopes to do better, but he begins his first day by spelling his name wrong. His friends think it's a joke. He is frustrated. Fortunately his perceptive new teacher realizes that Brian's problem is dyslexia. Testing, tutoring, and an effective educational plan reveal that Brian is not stupid, he just learns things in a different way. He builds on his interests with a project on the Canada goose. In the process Brian learns how to work with a girl who used to be his enemy, and he finds out that two of his pals are not such good friends after all. He also has to deal with his unsupportive father, who is also dyslexic. Though it seems unlikely that Brian's dyslexia wouldn't be diagnosed until the sixth grade, the issue is presented in a satisfying manner. Struggling students will relate to Brian's frustration, the discovery of his potential, and his understanding that learning in a different way is not necessarily bad.

Subjects: birds, dyslexia, learning disabled, middle school, self-perception, teachers

12 Birdseye, Tom. *Just Call Me Stupid*. Holiday House. 1993. Hardcover 181pp. Ages: 8–12. ISBN: 0–8234–1045–5 $16.95.

Patrick Lowe loved books and the idea of reading before he started school. But in first grade he got his letters all mixed up, kids stared at him, and his abusive father called him stupid. He had to go to the Resource Room for phonics worksheets and drills. It made him nervous, and he started to believe what his father had said. By the end of first grade the joy had gone out of books for Patrick. Now, in fifth grade, he still can't read. He still goes to the Resource Room for worksheets and drills, and he hates it. His regular classroom teacher, Mrs. Romero, wants to remove some of the pressure and let him stay in the classroom with other children where he can learn to enjoy books again. The reading resource teacher disagrees. Patrick is intelligent and imaginative. He runs away from the embarrassment of not being able to read by retreating into his own private world, The Kingdom, where he is the triumphant White Knight. He built The Kingdom in his backyard out of plywood, an orange crate, old concrete blocks, and cardboard. Patrick also likes to draw and is a talented artist. He is a good chess player, too. When a new girl, Celina, moves nextdoor, she discovers his Kingdom and wants to be his friend. She loves books, and her face glows when she reads. She reads to Patrick from *The Sword in the Stone,* and he, spellbound, becomes lost in the magic of the book. Celina thinks Patrick is really smart and encourages his drawing and storytelling gifts. She records Patrick telling a story, and without his knowing it, she submits it and his illustrations to a contest. His story is the prize-winning entry, and that means he has to read it aloud to the whole school. He becomes furious because he thinks he has been betrayed by Celina and because he can't read. But Celina doesn't give up on him. Neither does Mrs. Romero or his mother. Patrick realizes that their praise and support are justified. He is indeed the White Knight in The Kingdom. He is truthful and brave. He must fight to defend his honor, and he must fight to read. At the assembly, before the whole school, he panics at first. Then he feels strong and explains that he can't "read so great, . . . but (he) can tell (his story) pretty well." The next day he is allowed to stay in his regular classroom for reading and sit in the Reader's Chair. The book Mrs. Romero gives him to read is *The Sword in the Stone.* Some very funny scenes add to this novel about self-esteem and the pleasures of books.

Subjects: books and reading, elementary school, learning disabled, self-perception, special education

13 Blatchford, Claire. *Going with the Flow.* Lerner Publishing Group. 1998. Paperback 48pp. Ages: 8–12. ISBN: 1–5750–5284–9 $7.95. Illustrated by Janice Lee Porter.

On Mark's first day in his new fifth-grade class, he wonders if he is a freak. Everyone stares at him when the teacher introduces him as the new boy who can't hear. He is self-conscious about his hearing aids and is embarrassed by having an interpreter. No one knows sign language or understands how difficult it can be to read lips. Mark is indignant and lonely. His new classmates have never met a deaf student before and don't know how to act. The next day, at recess, Keith asks him to play basketball. Mark is a good ball player, and it is on the court that Mark and the others realize that they can communicate and be friends. Keith helps Mark to go with the flow. Mark joins the basketball team and begins teaching his teammates some sign language. The densely colored illustrations are heavy and often present children with featureless faces. Important information about deafness and sign language and advice on communicating with people who are deaf is included in an author's note.

Subjects: basketball, deaf, elementary school, physically handicapped, sign language, sports

14 Blatchford, Claire. *Nick's Secret* (A Nick Wilder Mystery). Lerner Publishing Group. 2000. Hardcover 168pp. Ages: 9–12. ISBN: 0–8225–0743–9 $14.95.

This novel in the Nick Wilder Mystery Series finds seventh-grader Nick in a suspenseful adventure that will appeal to dog lovers. Nick became deaf when he was in first grade and the nerves in his ears were damaged by meningitis. He feels he is especially quick at seeing things and keeping track of them. Daryl, an older, pot-selling bully, and his gang try to coerce Nick into using his heightened sensitivity to become a lookout for them. Sixteen-year-old Ionie comes to Nick's rescue with a rifle. Ionie is living alone with seven prize sheepdogs while her father is in Scotland with her dying grandfather. Meanwhile Daryl has stolen $350 from Ionie so she can't feed the dogs. And to make matters worse, there are dog thieves who will do anything to steal the dogs. All of this is Nick's secret until in the end his trusting mother, her boyfriend, and his boss at the pet store where he works all play an important part in the happy ending. The author of this series also lost her hearing at the age of six.

Subjects: bullies, deaf, dogs, middle school, physically handicapped

15 Bloor, Edward. *Tangerine*. Harcourt Brace & Co. 1997. Hardcover 294pp. Ages 12 and up. ISBN: 0–15–201246–X $17.00.

Living in surreal Tangerine, Florida, seventh-grader Paul Fisher has low vision, yet he is a successful soccer goalie. Bizarre natural disasters (houses repeatedly getting struck by lightning, underground fires rising through the muck, and portable classrooms being swallowed by sinkholes) actually do occur in this tangerine-growing region of Florida and make the setting for this novel intriguing. Paul's parents tell him that when he was little he was blinded by staring at an eclipse of the sun. Paul wears bottle-thick glasses and is bothered by the stigma attached to them. Adults in Paul's school and his parents recognize his visual impairment, but his peers do not seem aware of or concerned about his limited vision. Yet he sees better than most people. He sees the lies of his parents and begins to remember things about the incident that damaged his eyesight. As memories surface, Paul uncovers the terrifying truth about Erik, his older brother who is a football star. Paul ultimately wins acceptance in his new middle school where "minorities are in the majority," triumphs on the soccer team where some of the girls play better than any players he has seen before, learns valuable lessons by tending a freezing tangerine grove, and becomes a hero when he confronts his parents with the truth about his brother's violent behavior and involvement in the death of his friend's uncle. The several plot lines in this novel are smoothly blended, and the characters are vividly defined. Sports action, ecological horror, psychological suspense, and humorous middle-school scenes will hold the interest of young adult readers.

Subjects: Florida, middle school, physically handicapped, siblings, soccer, sports, visually handicapped

16   Booth, Barbara D. *Mandy*. Lothrop Lee & Shepard Books. 1991. Hardcover 32pp. Ages: 4–8. ISBN: 0–688–10338–3 $16.95. Illustrated by Jim La Marche.

When hearing-impaired Mandy visits her widowed Grandma, they have fun dancing, cooking, and walking in the woods. Mandy shares her perspective of the hearing world in which she lives as she wonders why people stop dancing when the radio stops, instead of when they feel like it, and how the sunlight sounds as it passes through the trees. On a country walk Grandma loses the special pin that Grandpa gave her on their twenty-fifth anniversary, and Mandy, despite her fear of the dark, later finds the pin. How things smell, feel, look, and taste to Mandy are described in vivid imagery and make readers think about how a deaf person and a hearing person use auditory cues differently to perceive their environments. The appealing illustrations realistically portray the two characters and give insight into Mandy's world. Her adventure is a good read-aloud for young children.

Subjects: deaf, grandparents, intergenerational relationships, physically handicapped

17   Bowler, Tim. *Midget*. Aladdin Paperbacks. 2000. Paperback 159pp. Ages: 12 and up. ISBN: 0–689–82909–4 $8.00.

Fifteen-year-old Midget is physically abnormal, speech-impaired, and subject to uncontrollable seizures. He is terrified of Seb, his seventeen-year-old brother, who blames him for their mother's death during childbirth. Midget's seizures are due to Seb's constant threats and nightly tortures of Midget. Sailing is Midget's only peace. He escapes to the wharf to watch Old Joseph restore an old wooden sailboat, called Miracle Man. Old Joseph understands Midget's desire to own the boat, and when the mysterious old sailor dies, the boat is willed to Midget. As Midget sails his own boat, he discovers that he can make things happen by visualizing them. He uses this ability to defeat Seb in two sailboat races and cause an accident that leaves Seb in a physical state similar to Midget's. Midget then realizes the meaning of Old Joseph's warning that miracles can be evil as well as good. He spares his brother but submits to Seb's girlfriend's plea to "sacrifice the part of you that hates until you love what you once hated" by walking off into the deepening sea. One of Midget's visits to a psychiatrist for biofeedback is integrated into the plot. This psychological thriller is imported from England and is set in Leigh-on-Sea. It is a fast-paced and spellbinding fantasy that offers a frightening look at sibling rivalry and abuse and raises complex questions about evil.

Subjects: abuse, boating, death, emotional problems, England, fantasy, mentally ill, physically handicapped, seizure disorder, siblings, speech disorders

18   Brooks, Bruce. *Vanishing*. Harper Collins. 1999. Paperback 103pp. Ages: 12 and up. ISBN: 0–06–447234–5 $6.95.

Eleven-year-old Alice is unwilling to live with her alcoholic mother and harsh stepfather. And her real-life dad prefers living without Alice. Hospitalized for bronchitis, she goes on a hunger strike so that she can stay in the hospital and not have to live in either impossible situation. In the hospital she develops an unusual relationship with Rex, an eleven-year-old boy with a terminal illness. He is tough-minded and outspoken. Wise beyond his years, he knows he is dying and offers Alice precocious advice. Alice grows weaker and weaker; six weeks into her "vanishing" she floats in and out of a hallucinating world, which is common to starvation. Psychological tests show that she does not have any clinical eating disorders, such as bulimia or anorexia nervosa. However, she is depressed. And she is technically malnourished and therefore cannot be discharged from the hospital. When Rex is close to death and the nurse won't let Alice visit him in intensive care, it is his words to her about giving up that make her decide to ask for food. She is allowed to see him before he dies. It is Rex who brings Alice to the realization that "all you get by giving up stuff is 'The Big Nothing.'" Largely written as conversation between Alice and Rex, this is a moving fable about an emotionally troubled preteen who makes a conscious decision to live.

Subjects: death, eating disorders, emotional problems, healthcare facilities, mentally ill

19   Brownridge, William Roy. *The Moccasin Goalie*. Orca Book Publishers. 1995. Paperback 32pp. Ages: 5–8. ISBN: 1–55143–054–1 $6.95. Illustrated by the author.

Inspired by Bill Brownridge, moccasin goalie for the 1952–53 Vawn Cougars ice hockey team in Canada, this first-person account tells the story of "Moccasin Danny" who can't wear skates because he has "a crippled leg and foot." His leather moccasins work fine. He lives for hockey, and he can slide across the goalmouth really fast. His fellow players and best friends include Anita with her long braids; big, quiet, and good skater Marcel; tough little Petou; and Danny's dog, Bingo. When winter and the chance to play real hockey finally arrive, the Wolves team players are announced. Only Marcel makes the team. Anita is cut because she is a girl, Petou is cut because he is too small, and Danny is cut because he can't skate. It is the biggest disappointment of his life. Weeks later, when a team member is hurt, the league gives Danny special permission to play in his moccasins. The Wolves win, and Danny can stay on the team. This exciting story about teamwork and not underestimating a child with a disability is brightened by gleaming color paintings of the icy Canadian winter.

Subjects: Canada, ice hockey, physically handicapped, sports

20   Buchanan, Dawna Lisa. *The Falcon's Wing*. Orchard Books. 1992. Hardcover 144pp. Ages: 10 and up. ISBN: 0–531–05986–3 $13.95.

After the death of her mother, twelve-year-old Bryn Cameron and her father move from Ohio to Ontario to stay temporarily with her mother's older sister, Pearl. Bryn's grieving father works hard on the farm and keeps to himself. Aunt Pearl, who is domineering, hard-hearted, and bossy, has a loving daughter, Winnie, who has Down syndrome. At first Bryn is frightened and aggravated by Winnie. She is embarrassed by her and has difficulty making new friends. They all tease Winnie, and so does Bryn. But the cousins' relationship grows. They become true friends. And it is Winnie who helps Bryn understand her family and adjust to her new life. This novel effectively deals with stages of grief and the treatment of a family member with Down syndrome.

Subjects: Canada, death, Down syndrome, grief, mentally handicapped

21   Butler, Geoff. *The Hangashore*. Tundra Books. 1998. Hardcover 32pp. Ages: 12 and up. ISBN: 0–88776–444–4 $17.99.

In Newfoundland a *hangashore* is defined as an unlucky fellow deserving pity, or a worthless person who is too lazy or unreliable to fish in the sea. World War II has just ended, and a new magistrate has been sent from England to a tiny fishing village to represent the government. The magistrate expects respect from everyone in the village, although he is too self-important to show any kindheartedness. He dislikes John Payne, the minister's sixteen-year-old son who has Down syndrome. John judges people not by their titles but by their actions. When the magistrate refuses to give up his pew in church for the returning soldiers, and John clashes with him by calling him a hangashore, he threatens to have the boy sent to a mental hospital. John, feeling like a hangashore himself, sails away in his father's fishing boat to hide. It takes a boating accident for the magistrate to realize John's abilities. He learns from John how to get along with people, that John's values are more meaningful than official titles, and that anyone can be a hangashore.

Geoff Butler is one of the Atlantic Provinces' best-known authors and artists, and his handsome oil paintings document the Newfoundland setting in this story about self-respect and acceptance.

Subjects: boating, Down syndrome, historical fiction, Newfoundland, self-perception, sports

22   Butts, Nancy. *Cheshire Moon*. Front Street Books. 1996. Hardcover 105pp. Ages: 9–12. ISBN: 1–886910–08–1 $14.95.

Twelve-year-old Miranda, who is hearing-impaired, is summering at her aunt's home on an island in Penobscot Bay. She is grieving her favorite cousin Timothy's mysterious death. Timothy was her best friend because he was the only hearing child to adjust to her disability. They communicated so well that her deafness was not an obstacle. After his drowning at sea, Miranda, feeling angry and isolated, refuses to speak. She only wants to read lips and sign, no matter how hard that makes it for her parents and teachers. She increasingly retreats from the hearing world. However, she does develop an awkward relationship with Boone, a fourteen-year-old boy who is employed by her aunt for odd jobs. He forces her to communicate and tries to lure her back to the real world. The plot turns mystical when the teens learn of the island legend of dreams becoming real during the smile of the Cheshire Moon. Miranda and Boone discover that they have recurring identical dreams about Timothy and a strange island. They wake to find sand, rockweed, and shells in their rooms. Miranda is eventually impelled to canoe across the windblown bay in the middle of the night to find Timothy and the sunken island, which has appeared in their dreams. She finds the island and Timothy but abandons him in order to rescue Boone, who has nearly drowned while swimming out in search of her. The story ends in August with a happier Miranda at her thirteenth birthday. The combination of reality and dreams is confusing and not logical. There are many loose ends. However, the author, a journalist who has worked with deaf children, perceptively depicts Miranda's feelings. Young readers who are deaf will relate to her loneliness, alienation, and unsureness. Hearing readers will learn about a deaf person's frustration living in a hearing world.

Subjects: boating, deaf, elective mutism, grief, physically handicapped, self-perception, sports

23   Caffrey, Jaye Andras. *First Star I See*. Verbal Images Press. 1997. Paperback 150pp. Ages: 8–12. ISBN: 1-884281-17-6 $9.95. Illustrated by Tracy L. Kane.

Paige Bradley has earned the reputation for being a "spacey" fourth grader. She daydreams, forgets her homework, and loses her school supplies. Paige has attention-deficit disorder (ADD) and is convinced that she is dumb. Her teachers, assistant principal Mr. Rodriguez, and her mother agree that she is smart and creative and has a very good imagination. Paige truly wants to win a writing contest at school so she can meet her favorite TV actress. Her best intentions fail. She can't check out research materials from the library because she has lost a library book and has missed two library days at school. And when she does try to write, she is too easily distracted. Mr. Rodriguez offers her his books on astronomy, but she must use them in his office during her recess. The books are not children's books, but Mr. Rodriguez is confident that she can handle them. Paige enjoys how Mr. Rodriguez talks to her like she is a grown-up. She finds the books interesting and draws pictures instead of taking notes. He suggests note taking and other tools to compensate for her ADD and to help her stay focused. Paige realizes the importance of his advice when she wins the contest by turning in the best report on stars, but she also loses the contest because she didn't follow the directions. She did not turn in an outline or a rough draft. Consequently she does not get to present her paper at the assembly and is heartbroken. But when the actress comes to school, she asks to meet Paige because she has a daughter who is being treated for ADD. Paige promises the actress that she will get help for her ADD. She knows that there is a lot of hard work ahead of her and that with the right tools she will learn to apply herself. Paige's brother adds a humorous note to the story. Mark is in kindergarten and has also been diagnosed with attention-deficit disorder. He calls it "tense and deaf to orders." Lists of books for young and older readers conclude this fast-moving adventure that is useful for children with ADD and for others who need to understand them.

Subjects: attention-deficit hyperactivity disorder, elementary school, learning disabled, siblings

24   Carter, Alden R. *Big Brother Dustin*. Albert Whitman and Co. 1997. Hardcover 32pp. Ages: 4–8. ISBN: 0–8075–0715–6 $14.95. Photos by Dan Young and Carol Alden.

Preschooler Dustin has Down syndrome, although it is never mentioned in the text. Dustin is thrilled at the wonderful news that his mom is going to have a baby girl. His parents suggest that maybe he can think of the perfect name for her. He comes up with a lot of ideas over the months while they get the baby's room ready and wait for her arrival. Dustin goes to a class at the hospital to learn how to be a big brother, but he still can't come up with the perfect name. Finally, a few days before his sister's birth, he decides to put together his grandmothers' names, Mary and Ann. Mary Ann is a name that makes everyone happy. Charming, color photographs extend the simple text and capture Dustin's joy at being Mary Ann's big brother. A snapshot album of Dustin and Mary Ann concludes this story about a boy with Down syndrome who experiences typical big brother emotions.

Subjects: Down syndrome, mentally handicapped, siblings

25   Carter, Alden R. *Dustin's Big School Day*. Albert Whitman & Co. 1999. Hardcover 32pp. Ages: 5–8. ISBN: 0–8075–1741–0 $14.95. Photos by Dan Young and Carol Carter.

Dustin, the star of *Big Brother Dustin*, who has Down syndrome, is in second grade now. As in *Big Brother Dustin*, his disability is not mentioned in this text. Today is a big school day because everyone is excited about their special assembly guests: Dave, a ventriloquist, and Skippy, his puppet. Otherwise it's a typical day. Dustin is mainstreamed into music, language arts, library, and science classes. He visits a speech therapist, an occupational therapist, and Mrs. Fadrowski, who helps special kids with their reading and arithmetic. His teachers creatively integrate information about Dave and Skippy into their regular lessons. At two o'clock Dave and Skippy arrive, put on an entertaining show, and stay to sign autographs. The natural, color photos and clear text depict the school environment of a special needs student.

Subjects: Down syndrome, elementary school, mentally handicapped, special education

26   Caseley, Judith. *Harry and Willy and Carrothead*. Greenwillow. 1991. Hardcover 24pp. Ages: 4–8. ISBN: 0–688–09492–9 $15.95. Illustrated by the author.

This story of a three-way friendship fosters self-respect among children despite physical differences. Harry is born with no left hand. At first his parents are sad and scared. Before they see what they have in their baby, they see what is missing. But Harry cries, coos, and waves his arms like any other baby. Harry's parents' attitude becomes very positive, and it helps Harry to be lively, confident, and a good ball player and friend. He is open in his responses to other children's questions about his prosthesis. His red-headed friend, Oscar, is not so confident. When another boy named Willy calls him "Carrothead," Harry defends Oscar and then the boys become good friends. The story is simply told because it is written by Oscar, who is the best writer in the class. The bright watercolor scenes include Harry finger-painting great designs with his hand and his arm, the boys' multicultural school setting, charming Halloween party costumes, and a final portrait of the three boys who are different and also very alike.

Subjects: elementary school, physically handicapped, self-perception

27   Christopher, Matt (Hirschfeld, Robert). *Fighting Tackle*. Little, Brown. 1995. Paperback 147pp. Ages: 8–12. ISBN: 0–316–13794–4 $3.95. Illustrated by Karin Lidbeck.

Terry McFee, whose age is never given, is a football player who has been assigned a new position on his team. He has trouble accepting the fact that he is not as fast as he once was. He is now stronger and bigger and has been switched to offensive tackle. Terry must also deal with the fact that his younger brother, Nicky, who was born with Down syndrome and is training for the Special Olympics, is a faster runner. Also adding to the tension between the brothers is Terry's embarrassment when Nicky cheers him on when he's on the football field. Terry works hard and becomes successful in his new position. And Nicky becomes a talented runner. When their father is injured in a truck accident, the boys have to work together. Terry says that he's not half the runner Nicky is and convinces him to run for help. Five black-and-white drawings that capture the action and lengthy football scenes will appeal to young sports fans. A brief description of Down syndrome is offered in this easy-to-read sports story with a realistic portrayal of a Down syndrome child.

Subjects: Down syndrome, football, mentally handicapped, siblings, Special Olympics, sports

28   Christopher, Matt (Hirschfeld, Robert). *Wheel Wizards*. Little, Brown. 2000. Paperback 120pp. Ages: 9–12. ISBN: 0–316–13733–2 $4.50.

Twelve-year-old Seth Pender is angry and confused and thinks he can no longer play basketball because he was the victim of a horrible car accident that left him in a wheelchair for life. He is glum, uncommunicative, and unresponsive to his family, friends, and therapist. When he meets Danny, who plays wheelchair basketball, he becomes enthralled and realizes that he can be an athlete again. He sets goals, works hard, and copes with an extremely demanding coach. He learns to focus on what he's capable of doing and less on what happened and his rotten break. His coach's message, "You all need to be independent as possible," finally makes sense to him, and he becomes a star wheelchair basketball player. This fast-paced sports novel teaches that life is all about taking challenges and meeting them. It also contains interesting information about the sport and the specialized wheelchairs used by the players.

Subjects: basketball, middle school, physically handicapped, sports, wheelchair basketball, wheelchairs

29   Condra, Estelle. *See the Ocean*. Ideals Children's Books. 1994. Hardcover 32pp. Ages: 5–8. ISBN: 1–57102–005–5 $14.95. Illustrated by Linda Crockett-Blassingame.

Nellie, who is blind, loves the ocean. As a baby she wiggled her toes in the waves. As a toddler she touched shells and seaweed and fed crumbs to the seagulls. She listened to her parents when they answered her endless questions about the ocean. Now it is time for the family's annual trip to their beach house. Her competitive brothers play games in the car and have a contest to see who can be first to see the ocean. Nellie sits quietly, listening. This year, a heavy mist keeps them from seeing the ocean. But Nellie claims to see it first. She delivers a very romantic three-paragraph description of the ocean as an old man with his crown of pearls, shoes of shells, and cloak sprinkled with moons and stars. When her brother complains that she couldn't possibly see the ocean, their mother concludes that even though Nellie is blind, she can see with her mind. The author, who is blind, offers careful sensory details of sights, sounds, and textures of the beach, helping readers see in a deeper way. And the illustrator always covers Nellie's eyes with a wide-brimmed hat. The text is placed in semi-transparent panels on the unfocused, misty oil paintings that convey the beauty of Nellie's ocean world.

Subjects: blind, nature, physically handicapped, siblings

30   Covington, Dennis. *Lizard*. Delacorte Press. 1991. Hardcover 198pp. Ages: 12 and up. ISBN: 0–385–30307–6 $15.00.

Thirteen-year-old Lucius Sims is nicknamed Lizard because his facial deformity makes him look like a reptile. His guardian, Miss Colley, puts him in the Leesville Louisiana State School for Retarded Boys, even though there is no evidence that he is mentally handicapped. There he meets an interesting assortment of disabled characters and discovers that the school is no place for him. A traveling actor named Callahan comes to the school to perform *Treasure Island* and claims that he is Lizard's father. Lizard knows his father is dead but regards Callahan as his chance to escape and see the world. They journey with a troupe of down-and-out actors to Birmingham, where Lizard plays Caliban in *The Tempest*. Along the way he makes friends with Sammy and Rain, two black kids who live alone in a pump house, a museum curator, and a black artist. He learns that the adult world can be rough and unfair to young outcasts. He finds his real self and eventually returns to Miss Cooley, who turns out to be his mother. Lizard is a curious character on a madcap adventure who knows that the way he looks is only the outward sign that he is different.

Subjects: African Americans, facial disfiguration, physically handicapped, self-perception, special education, theatre

31   Cowen-Fletcher, Jane. *Mama Zooms*. Scholastic. 1996. Paperback 30pp. Ages: 5–8. ISBN: 0–590–48775–6 $4.99. Illustrated by the author.

In this simple, easy-to-read story for beginning readers, a young boy and his wheelchair-mobile mama have exciting adventures. Her wheelchair is a "zooming machine" when he sits on her lap and she zooms him everywhere. He imagines himself a jockey, a sea captain, a racecar driver, a pilot, a train engineer, a cowboy, and more. The wheelchair is manually operated, and Mama has very strong arms from all the zooming. The boy helps Daddy push her up only the very steepest hills. Mama zooms him right up to bedtime, and that's when he likes her best. Full-page, soft pastel and colored pencil drawings with crisp outlines add warmth to the very special relationship Mama and her son share. No disability is mentioned in the text. The story was inspired by the author's sister who is a wheelchair mom and practicing veterinarian.

Subjects: physically handicapped, wheelchairs

32   Creel, Ann Howard. *Water at the Blue Earth*. Roberts Rinehart Publishers (Boulder, CO). 1998. Hardcover 143pp. Ages: 9–12. ISBN: 1–57098–209–0 $14.95.

In 1854, twelve-year-old Wren Taylor and her parents move from Boston to Fort Massachusetts in New Mexico Territory to begin a new life on the frontier. Wren is one of only a few children who live at the outpost. She attends school there but doesn't make friends easily. She gradually befriends Luther, a blind Ute boy who is sent to the school to learn English. Wren's first opinions of Luther are rather poor, but as she comes to know him better she recognizes that her earlier opinions were formed because she feared someone so different. They explore the territory together and learn about each other's cultures. She also learns about the blind boy's special abilities to listen to the Earth, and by using some vivid imagery she also teaches Luther about colors. When war breaks out and Wren hears of the planned attack against Luther's peaceful people, she faces an anguishing decision. Should she follow her father's orders to keep quiet, or should she warn Luther of the upcoming attack? Courageous Wren makes the crucial decision to warn Luther's people and makes a dangerous journey to accomplish her task. A foreword, written by an authority on the history and culture of the territory, an epilogue, and an author's note offer enriching historical facts and attest to the accurate portrayal of the white and Native American characters in this engaging story. A list of suggested readings is also included.

Subjects: blind, historical fiction, Native Americans, New Mexico, physically handicapped

33   Crofford, Emily. *When the River Ran Backward* (Adventures in Time Series). Lerner Publishing Group. 2000. Paperback 84pp. Ages: 9–12. ISBN: 1-57505-488-4 $6.95.

This brief novel belongs to the Adventures in Time series. It is 1811, near the Mississippi River town of New Madrid, in the part of the Louisiana Territory that is now Missouri. Fifteen-year-old Laurel and her family are among the first white settlers in the area. Laurel was born with a harelip and is self-conscious about it. She worries that she will never marry because her mouth is unkissable. On December 16 the first in a sequence of violent earthquakes strikes. Laurel's family home is devastated, and many of their animals are killed. The community suffers through weeks of hardship, works together, and survives. An unexpected romance helps Laurel overcome her self-doubt about her disability. A map of the United States and its territories, as well as a prologue, set the scene for the story; and an afterword gives facts about earthquakes in Missouri that killed thousands of people and actually made parts of the river run in different directions.

Subjects: harelip, historical fiction, Missouri

34   Crutcher, Chris. *Staying Fat for Sarah Byrnes*. Bantam Doubleday Dell Books. 1993. Paperback 216pp. Ages: 12 and up. ISBN: 0-440-219-6-X $4.99.

At the age of three Sarah Byrnes, now seventeen, had her face deliberately burned on a hot wood stove by her brutal and psychotic father, Virgil. Virgil, who is "off the charts scary," refused to let her have reconstructive surgery, saying that her condition would teach her to "be tough." Consequently she has lived behind a mask of scars and anger. Headstrong, she is "the toughest person in our solar system." Eric Calhoune is a high school senior, known as Moby because of his excessive weight and swimming ability. Both Sarah and Moby share "terminal uglies" and are social outcasts. He is the fattest kid in school and she is the ugliest, but they are both among the brightest. Because of the strict workouts of competitive swimming, Moby loses weight, and this threatens his treasured friendship with Sarah. He overeats to stay fat in order not to jeopardize it. But Sarah reassures him that he has nothing to worry about. Now, Sarah abruptly stops talking, withdraws from the world, and is institutionalized in the Sacred Heart psychiatric ward. Moby visits her there every day. He talks to her, trying to get her to respond. And when she finally answers, she tells him she has been aware all along and just needed some time off. She is not speaking so she can stay in the hospital, safe from her unbalanced, wicked father, who is getting crazy again. Moby finally brings in Cynthia Lemry, his sympathetic swimming coach and English teacher, to protect Sarah and to help search for Sarah's mother. Sarah's mother abandoned her shortly after the barn "accident" and is the only person who can tell the truth about what Sarah's father did to her. Sarah and Mrs. Lemry travel to Reno to find her mother, but her mother is still a coward. She won't help. Meanwhile Virgil threatens to kill Moby unless he tells where Sarah is, and in a violent attack he stabs Moby with a hunting knife and then escapes. Eventually Virgil is found guilty in superior court and is sentenced to more than twenty years in prison. Moby gets a scholarship to swim at a small National Association of Intercollegiate Athletics (NAIA) college, and Sarah gets new and caring parents when Cynthia Lemry and her husband sign formal adoption papers for her. Sarah plans on attending the community college until she decides what to do with her life. The daily Contemporary American Thought class discussions about the existence of God, abortion, organized religion, and suicide serve as a backdrop for the story and bring life to today's teen world. A sophisticated plot, extraordinary characters, difficult and serious situations, black humor, and vivid language move this gripping story, which is about the true nature of courage, along at top speed.

Subjects: abuse, burn injuries, elective mutism, facial disfiguration, healthcare facilities, high school, overweight, self-perception, sports, swimming

35 Crutcher, Chris. *Whale Talk*. Greenwillow Books. 2001. Hardcover 220pp. Ages: 12 and up. ISBN: 0–688–18019–1 $15.95.

T.J. (The Tao) Jones is racially mixed and adopted. He is an academically gifted senior and a former Junior Olympics swimmer at Cutter High School in central Washington. Until this year he stayed away from organized sports in school. But now his English teacher, Mr. Simet, asks for help in starting up a swim team. The school does not have a pool or any other competitive swimmers. However, T.J. sees this as an opportunity to make a statement about the way the establishment worships organized athletics. He purposely recruits guys who would look the most out of place in Cutter's sacred blue and gold letter jackets. "Never in the history of Cutter High School has a team of this diversity been assembled." There's Simon DeLong, who weighs 287 pounds, and Jackie Craig, a nondescript chameleon who rarely speaks. Andy Mott is a surly psychopath, the king of in-school and out-of-school suspension, who surprises everyone at the first practice by unstrapping his right leg. No one knew he has a prosthesis from just above the knee. Tay-Roy Kibble is a body builder and a musician. Girls love him.

And T.J. also recruits mentally handicapped Chris Coughlin and a gifted student, Dan Hole, two extremes on the intellectual scale. High school has offered little to his team of real outsiders, a "Team Bizzaro." They train at All Night Fitness in the only indoor pool in town, which is only twenty yards with four lanes. No teams will come there for meets, so T.J.'s swimmers are a perennial road team. They work hard and become very dedicated to each other. Their bus rides to swim meets become informal therapy sessions where the misfits bond. They face many obstacles during the year, but in the end they triumph. The seven outcasts set a goal, meet it, now have friends, and look at life in a different way. T.J. is an energetic hero who is confident and wise for his age. His adoptive mother, a lawyer who deals with child abuse cases, and his adoptive father, a Guardian ad Litem who represents children in child abuse cases in juvenile court, contribute much to T.J.'s strong character. Subplots concern racism, child abuse, realistic high school issues, and shocking tragedies. The author writes from his personal experience as a family therapist and a child protection specialist.

Subjects: adoption, African Americans, Asians, gifted and talented, high school, mentally handicapped, overweight, physically handicapped, popularity, self-perception, sports, swimming

36 Cummings, Priscilla. *A Face First.* Dutton. 2001. Hardcover 197pp. Ages: 12 and up. ISBN: 0–525–46522–7 $16.99.

When sixth-grader Kelley wakes up in a hospital burn unit with third-degree burns to her face, leg, and hand, she can't remember the details of the car accident and resulting fire that melted her small frog earring and much of her skin. She endures multiple skin-graft operations, debridement, hand exercises, a pressure glove and stocking, and a clear plastic facemask that she has to wear for a year while new skin forms. Her anger, confusion, and depression lead her to withdraw from the world. She wonders why the catastrophe had to happen to her, if her mother is at fault for the accident, and who she (Kelley) is now that her appearance has been dramatically changed. She rejects her friends and is determined not to return to school in the fall. In her struggle to recover, Kelley discovers her inner strength and a talent for drawing that she didn't know she had. She meets a fellow burn victim and realizes that she is not alone. She learns that she has to direct attention away from the burn and the mask to the person inside and let her personality shine through. She also learns the importance of second impressions. The author is a former newspaper and magazine writer who has researched burn injuries and accurately and authentically describes burn unit procedures in this fast-paced novel.

Subjects: art, burn injuries, facial disfiguration, healthcare facilities, mentally ill, self-perception

37   Cutler, Jane. *Spaceman*. Puffin Books. 1999. Paperback 138pp. Ages: 8–12. ISBN: 0–14–038150–3 $4.99.

Ten-year-old Gary Harris is getting an F in everything he does in fifth grade and doesn't know how to try any harder. His teacher accuses him of being lazy and careless and of not paying attention. Gary's father angrily blames Gary's teachers for Gary's problems. Furthermore, his father doesn't think that being able to read is important anymore. Everything is on TV or video or the computer. He gets along just fine and he never reads a thing. In first grade Gary liked to read, but now he hates books. He doesn't get along with his classmates because they think he's too big, too clumsy, and too stupid. He copes with all the pressure by spacing out, moving "into a place of his own where nobody else could go." Kids call him "space case, space cadet, spaceout, spacy and spaceman." Gary has spent time in the full-time special education class in his school, but now because he has injured another student he is sent to the county Special Needs class. With the help of his knowledgeable and understanding teacher, Mrs. Block, Gary blossoms in his new special education classroom. Mrs. Block watches Gary carefully to discover what's best for him. She finds out that he is an auditory learner, that he has trouble with spatial orientation, and that he is dyslexic. She provides ways to help him. He makes friends with Jesse, who is always running away, and with Amanda, who lets him help her train a puppy to be a guide dog. Gary works at his own pace, his skills and self-esteem improve, and he no longer needs to "space out." Mrs. Block is optimistic. She describes him as kind, helpful, and cooperative. He completes his assignments and earns A's, B's, and gold stars. Gary is learning. The accurate descriptions of how it looks and feels to have a special learning style and an inside view of a special education classroom heighten awareness and understanding of students like Gary.

Subjects: dogs—service, dyslexia, elementary school, emotional problems, learning disabled, self-perception, service dogs, special education, teachers

38   Dahl, Roald. *The Vicar of Nibbleswicke*. Puffin Books. 1994. Paperback 45pp. Ages: 9–12. ISBN: 0–14–036837–X. Out of print. Illustrated by Quentin Blake.

This imaginative look at dyslexia is classic Roald Dahl craziness with illustrations by Britain's Children's Laureate Quentin Blake. It was written for the Dyslexia Institute, and all rights, worldwide, for the period of copyright, have been donated for the benefit of the Institute. According to the story, when the Reverend Lee was a boy he suffered from severe dyslexia. Guided by the Dyslexia Institute of London and his teachers, his reading and writing improved, he trained as a minister, and he became the vicar of Nibbleswicke. Taking up his new duties, he gets nervous and develops a very peculiar illness. It is not dyslexia, but it is related in some way. When speaking, he reverses words. For example, *God* becomes *dog*, *pastor* becomes *rotsap*, and so on. The entire village is convinced that he is "completely and utterly barmy." After a stream of hysterical reversals, the local doctor diagnoses the vicar's problem. It's Back-to-Front Dyslexia, which "is very common among tortoises, who . . . call themselves esio-trots." The cure involves walking backwards while speaking. The problem with this is that the vicar can't see where he is going. So he attaches a small rear-view mirror to his forehead, and the congregation grows to love the eccentric man. This short story is a delightful read-aloud.

Subjects: dyslexia, England, learning disabled

39   Damrell, Liz. *With the Wind*. Orchard Books. 1991. Hardcover 32pp. Ages: 5–8. ISBN: 0–531–05882–4. Out of print. Illustrated by Stephen Marchesi.

This prose poem and the action-filled oil paintings capture the freedom experienced by a young boy riding a horse. The flowing manes and tails, the powerful pounding hooves, and the wind whipping the boy's hair illustrate what this Rider of Horses feels as he "sits in the air" and senses "the earth move away." "He's alive to the sounds, the sights, the smells, the feel of the horse's life." On the final two pages the significance of the ride is revealed. Here, the boy in braces is lifted off the horse and pushed away in a wheelchair. Changing perspectives in the illustrations impart life to the freedom and strength that riding gives the boy.

Subjects: horses, physically handicapped, wheelchairs

40   Davis, Patricia. *Brian's Bird*. Albert Whitman & Co. 2000. Hardcover 32pp. Ages: 5–9. ISBN 0–8075–0881–0 $14.95. Illustrated by Layne Johnson.

Author Patricia Davis was a teacher of visually impaired children, and this story was inspired by one of her students. Brian is a blind boy who delights in the parakeet he receives for his eighth birthday. He names the bird Scratchy because of the way it feels on his finger. His using his sense of touch to explore the wire and his listening to the bird call his name help young readers understand the special skills of a blind person. When Brian's older brother carelessly leaves the front door open, Scratchy flies away. By working together the boys find Scratchy, coax him onto Brian's finger, and bring him home to safety. This simple, well-written story features an affectionate African American family. Johnson's brightly colored illustrations capture the boys' emotions and present good images of the bird from some unusual perspectives.

Subjects: African Americans, birds, blind, physically handicapped, siblings

41 Dessen, Sarah. *Keeping the Moon*. Puffin Books. 1999. Paperback 228pp. Ages: 12 and up. ISBN: 0–14–131007–3 $5.99.

Colie Sparks is spending her fifteenth summer in Colby, North Carolina, with her eccentric Aunt Mira. Colie's mother is aerobics star and "weightloss evangelist" Kiki Sparks, who is touring Europe. Kiki once weighed 325 pounds. Now she is famous for infomercials, the Kiki Buttmaster, Kiki-eats, Flykiki videos, and fitness wear. Colie, too, has lost a lot of weight and looks great. But she hasn't lost her negative self-image. She is still haunted by whispers and taunts of "Lard-O" and "Thunder Thighs." She feels like she is wearing a permanent "Kick Me" sign at home and school and in the rest of the world. She reacts by shutting down, retreating, and sporting dyed black hair and a lip ring. Aunt Mira, though she wears outlandish clothes and is fat, has a positive self-image, which does influence Colie. Colie gets a job at the Last Chance Café, where she befriends fellow waitresses Morgan and Isabel. They give Colie a makeover and help her see her potential. And sweet, seventeen-year-old Norman, the hippie-artist who lives in Mira's basement, paints a portrait of Colie. She feels his smiles "all the way to (her) toes." Aunt Mira, Morgan, Isabel, and Norman all offer Colie the wisdom and support she needs to let go of the "fat years" and to believe in herself. The sharp dialogue, realistic characters, and positive message allow teens to identify with outcast Colie and her caterpillar-to-butterfly metamorphosis.

Subjects: overweight, self-perception

42 Dobkin, Bonnie. *Just a Little Different*. Children's Press. 1994. Hardcover 32pp. Ages: 4–8. ISBN: 0–516–02018–8 $18.00. Illustrated by Keith Neely.

A young black girl introduces her best friend, Josh, who uses a wheelchair. She explains how they are alike. They both love school, monster movies, and computers. They play catch and listen to the same music. But they are also different. She walks and he zooms. She uses stairs and Josh rolls down ramps. She concludes that she and Josh are a lot alike and just a little different. The watercolor illustrations show the children in school and at play. A word list is included at the end of this Rookie Reader.

Subjects: African Americans, physically handicapped, wheelchairs

43 Dodds, Bill. *My Sister Annie*. Boyds Mills Press. 1993. Hardcover 92pp. Ages: 8–12. ISBN: 1–56397–114–3 $7.95.

Twelve-year-old Charlie has four challenges to face before he graduates from elementary school. First, he desperately wants to join the cool middle-school club called the Bombers. Charlie knows right from wrong and has difficulty with the club's prankish initiation activities. Second, he has to pitch his best baseball game in order to win the league championship, but he has a hard time concentrating. Third, he hopes to go to the school dance with Misty, but he can't quite summon the courage to ask her. His fourth and toughest challenge is Annie, his older sister who has Down syndrome. Annie complicates every part of his life. He loves and resents her. The fact that he doesn't even want his peers to know about her makes him feel mad, bad, and guilty. Charlie is a thoughtful character, and in the end he gets involved in a sibling's group for kids his age who have a brother or sister with some kind of disability. He's still confused about a lot of things, but he's sure of one thing: He loves Annie. Charlie's parents are well intentioned, and their name game with his four-year-old identical twin sisters adds lightheartedness to the book. They are really named Rhoda and Rhonda but are called by any two things that go together. Clever combinations include Rock and Roll, Salt and Pepper, and Pots and Pans. Smoothly integrated into Charlie's first-person narrative are facts about Down syndrome.

Subjects: baseball, Down syndrome, elementary school, mentally handicapped, siblings, sports, twins

44 Dorris, Michael. *Sees Behind Trees*. Hyperion. 1996. Paperback 128pp. Ages: 9–12. ISBN: 0–7868–1357–1 $4.99.

Set in sixteenth-century America, this short novel tells how a young Powhatan boy turns his sight impairment into an advantage and becomes an adult. Because Walnut cannot see well, he fears his coming-of-age ceremony, which involves feats with a bow and arrow. At the ceremony the boys are asked to listen to the woods and "see" what cannot be seen. Walnut's highly developed hearing allows him to proclaim the approach of Gray Fire, the elderly artist, and earns him his adult name, Sees Behind Trees. He then embarks on a journey with Gray Fire to find the mysterious land of water. On their journey they encounter friendly strangers and many dangers. Sees Behind Trees survives alone in the snow and also rescues a baby. He returns to his village with the wisdom that his journey will continue. This tale is richly told in the first person and creates a strong sense of culture. Sounds and scents are vividly portrayed. Middle-school students will recognize similarities between the experiences of Sees Behind Trees and their own rights and responsibilities despite the temporal and cultural differences.

Subjects: blind, historical fiction, intergenerational relationships, Native Americans, nature, physically handicapped

45   Dowell, Frances O'Rourke. *Dovey Coe*. Atheneum. 2000. Hardcover 181pp. Ages: 9 and up. ISBN: 0–689–83174–9 $16.00.

It's 1928 in Indian Creek, North Carolina, and twelve-year-old Dovey Coe is being tried for Parnell Caraway's murder. It all started when wealthy, vicious, and greedy Parnell set his sights on Dovey's beautiful older sister and tried to destroy her dreams of escaping small-town life and going to teacher's college. Parnell abuses Dovey and her thirteen-year-old brother, Amos, who is deaf. Irrepressible Dovey is not afraid to say what she thinks, even when it gets her into trouble. She has good reason because she's always had to stick up for Amos, who folks misunderstand because he is deaf. She taught him how to read books and lips. Older and wiser characters refuse to see that Amos is highly attuned to the world around him. Dovey is strong willed, stubborn, and sweet. This feisty heroine always speaks the truth. On page one she states, "I hated Parnell Caraway as much as the next person, but I didn't kill him." Southern courtroom drama and an inexperienced city lawyer lead to Dovey having to solve the murder herself. Dovey's mountain twang brings the setting to life in this fascinating, fast-paced story about love, hate, and the pursuit of truth.

Subjects: deaf, historical fiction, mystery, physically handicapped, siblings

46   Doyle, Malachy. *Georgie*. Bloomsbury Publishing Plc (London). 2001. Paperback 155pp. Ages: 12 and up. ISBN: 0–7475–5154–5   £5.99.

Fourteen-year-old Georgie hides many secrets. He is alienated from himself and his surroundings. He is often violent. He does not speak or communicate at all. When he is moved to a special school in Wales, he sees it as an opportunity for a fresh start. He believes that deep down he's not that different. He wants to do what other teens do and be happy. He likes Tommo, his new teacher, who is very perceptive. Tommo knows just what to do to help Georgie overcome his fears and to be good. Shannon, a girl who is Georgie's age and a resident in the special school, also reaches out to Georgie. She draws smiling faces and rivers for him and represents the River Shannon in Ireland, a source of strength and hope for Georgie. Georgie slowly remembers the events of seven years ago when his mother was murdered and accepts what happened in his past. He finally moves forward out of his depression and speaks. This powerful story of Georgie's inner struggle is written in alternating first-person narratives of Georgie and Shannon.

Subjects: art, elective mutism, grief, mentally ill, middle school, special education, teachers

47 Edwards, Becky. *My Brother Sammy*. Millbrook Press. 1999. Hardcover 32pp. Ages: 4–8. ISBN: 0–7613–0439–8 $15.00. Illustrated by David Armitage.

Sammy is an autistic child who does things differently than his brother does. The story is told from the brother's point of view. The brother is sad when Sammy can't go to school in the car with him because Sammy goes to a different school. He is embarrassed when Sammy doesn't join in the games he plays with his friends. He is lonely when Sammy doesn't build sand castles with him. He is frustrated when Sammy can't talk to him. And he is angry when Sammy knocks down the tallest tower of blocks he has ever built. Mom explains that Sammy is his special brother and that he is Sammy's special brother. Sammy turns the tables here, and the two boys play together. The brother experiences things Sammy's way. He is happy to have a special brother because that makes him special, too. The lyrical text is matched by misty watercolor illustrations in this sensitively written story about brotherly love.

Subjects: autism, elementary school, siblings, special education

48 Eliot, Eve. *Insatiable: The Compelling Story of Four Teens, Food, and Its Power*. Health Communications Inc. 2001. Paperback 284pp. Ages: 12 and up. ISBN: 1–55874–818–0 $12.95.

This compelling novel is about four teens and their relationships with food. Samantha is outwardly perfect. She's a beautiful, thin cheerleader whose boyfriend breaks up with her because she doesn't eat and is too concerned about her weight. Being neat and tidy are so important to her that she constantly vacuums her room. And she cuts herself as punishment for eating. She is soothed by the pain. Hannah binges on account of grief over the death of her mother. She throws up the huge amounts of food she eats when she is alone. Jessica is an artist who starves herself to death. Her father has died from AIDS, and she has to take care of her little brother because her actress mother is rarely home. Phoebe is the smartest and fattest girl in school. Her father is a professional photographer who works with thin models and pressures Phoebe to lose weight. She wants to be loved for her "Phoebe-ness" and not because she is thin. Phoebe and Jessica are friends from the start. They meet Samantha and Hannah at group therapy. Their therapist is perceptive and determined, and through their sessions the girls' pain, fears, confusion, and courage are revealed. All, except Jessica, discover that they are not alone and that recovery is possible. Written as character-driven episodes, the girls' stories are woven together in a descriptive and sensitive style. The author, who herself has suffered from and overcome anorexia, compulsive eating, and obesity, is a psychotherapist and an expert in the field of treating food addiction. An afterword suggests ways for teens to get help with their eating disorders and gives the author's e-mail address.

Subjects: art, eating disorders, emotional problems, grief, mentally ill, overweight, self-perception

49 Farrell, Mame. *Marrying Malcolm Murgatroyd*. Farrar, Straus & Giroux. 1998. Paperback 121pp. Ages: 9–12. ISBN: 0–374–44744–6 $4.95.

Twelve-year-old Hannah Billings is a cool sixth grader, one of the Popular Kids. Yet she struggles to fit in because the biggest nerd in the class, Malcolm Murgatroyd, is the son of her parents' best friends. Their families have even projected their marriage since they were born. And her third-grade brother, Ian, has muscular dystrophy. Malcolm is too studious, has greasy hair, and is always a year behind in sneakers. Everyone makes fun of Malcolm. But he is Ian's supporter and close friend. He is the only person who can cheer Ian up. Hannah has to hide her friendship with Malcolm, also known as Murgadork, so her friends don't think she's a geek. She dreads her school autobiographical scrapbook project because her friends will find out how much of her life has included Malcolm. When Ian is rushed to the hospital with respiratory failure, Malcolm is there. He is strong, rational, and brave. Hannah sees Malcolm's true personality and confronts her conflicts about guilt and loyalty. Back in school, she reads her autobiography aloud to her class and publicly acknowledges the importance of both boys in her life. The final sentence in the book, which shifts tense, is a bit of a surprise. Malcolm is a well-drawn character. He seems to enjoy being weird but also feels pain when he is shunned. He is a free thinker with a strong spirit. Hannah's dilemmas about Malcolm's friendship and Ian's disability are treated without sentimentality. With snappy dialogue and touching moments, this is a believable story about strength, courage, and friendship.

Subjects: elementary school, middle school, muscular dystrophy, physically handicapped, popularity, self-perception

50   Fellman, Wilma R. *The Other Me: Poetic Thoughts on ADD for Adults, Kids, and Parents*. Special Press. 1997. Paperback 121pp. Ages: 9 and up. ISBN: 1–886941–16–5 $16.00. Illustrated by Arnold C. Fellman.

This book of poems is a sensitive, lighter look at the attention-deficit disorder experience. "Embraceable You" encourages individuals with ADD to give up feeling hopeless and, like Walt Whitman, celebrate themselves. The restlessness, distractibility, and forgetfulness of a person with ADD are addressed in "Block It Out. "Lima Beans, Broccoli, and Liver" humorously describes the anxiety of an eleven-year-old girl when her teacher calls on her. "Tails from the Silver Screen" suggests that what we need in this life is a script to follow but then questions, "Did someone forget to send me a script?" In "5, 4, 3, 2, 1. . ." the clash between a parent and an ADD child starts out with chaos and ends in love and understanding. The author, who is a licensed professional counselor and former teacher, shares the frustrations of ADD and lifts the burden with laughter in this unique collection. Information about attention-deficit disorders and a list of suggested references are included. Black-and-white illustrations of a squirrtle playfully complement the selections. A squirrtle represents the ADD individual and is an animal that acts lively like a squirrel and pulls in like a turtle.

Subjects: attention-deficit hyperactivity disorder, elementary school, learning disabled, poetry

51   Fenner, Carol. *Yolonda's Genius*. Margaret K. McElderry Books. 1995. Hardcover 211pp. Ages: 9 and up. ISBN: 0–689–80001–0 $17.00.

Fifth-grader Yolonda and her first-grader brother, Andrew, move to a small Michigan town with their momma to get away from the crime and drugs in their Chicago school. Yolonda is cool, smart, and a great big girl. At first she doesn't like her new town. She misses Grant Park, the Art Institute, and the lively Chicago noise. She is taunted for being overweight, but she loves to eat and doesn't apologize for it. Andrew is small, doesn't talk much, and has to attend a special reading class for slow learners. He can't make sense of the black marks that march across the page, the "code people used instead of talking." Looking at those marks hurts his head. What Andrew loves to do is play the harmonica given to him as a baby by his father. He can imitate bacon sizzling, people's voices, and any sound he hears. He can also express his moods and emotions. Yolonda understands that music is the way Andrew "talks." She knows he is a musical genius and tries to convince others of his strong musical intelligence. On a visit back to Chicago for the annual blues festival, Yolonda's plans fall into line and Andrew's musical gift is recognized. Other characters in this Newbery Honor Book who come to life are Aunt Tiny and Vic Watts. Yolonda's Aunt Tiny owns three famous hairdressing salons in Chicago. She weighs over 300 pounds, and her size adds to her character. Her extra poundage is celebrated rather than insulted. She "gloriously" fills the doorway, has to sit in three seats on the airplane, and has a "laugh as rich and flaky as biscuits and gravy." Vic Watts, Andrew's speech therapist who stutters, understands that the music-writing code, which Andrew calls Mickey Mouse shoes on sticks, makes more sense to Andrew than the word-writing code. He listens when Andrew speaks through his harmonica and helps him learn to read by teaching that *A* is for *accordion* and *B* is for *bongo*, and so on. This warm and inspiring story about an African American family moves to a satisfying yet somewhat unbelievable conclusion.

Subjects: African Americans, Chicago, dyslexia, elementary school, gifted and talented, learning disabled, music, overweight, physically handicapped, siblings, special education, speech disorders, teachers

52 Ferris, Jean. *Of Sound Mind.* Farrar, Straus & Giroux. 2001. Hardcover 215pp. Ages: 12 and up. ISBN: 0–374–35580–0 $16.00.

Theo is a high school senior who is especially good at math. He is the only "hearie" in his family and he feels suspended, hanging between the hearing and deaf worlds. He is an automatic, live-in interpreter who is at his family's constant disposal. Theo's mother, Palma, is a successful sculptor and a domineering, self-absorbed primadonna. Theo has to make her phone calls and act as her business manager. Jeremy is Theo's dependent younger brother who relies on Theo for companionship and fifth-grade homework help. Theo's father, Thomas, is a furniture maker who has never really burdened his son. "His hands were his lifeline: the way he communicated, made his living, expressed his humor and his creativity, showed his love." Theo is exhausted by his position in his family and loaded with conflict, resentment, and guilt. He meets fascinating Ivy, who has big dark eyes and a purple streak in her hair. Ivy knows how to sign because her father is deaf. Theo becomes wrapped up in a romance with Ivy, her after-school catering business, and her model-building, Ph.D. father. He opens up to her. He explains how "other" he feels, and how anxious, worried, and scared to death he is. However, Theo and Ivy don't always agree. When Theo's father suffers a stroke, Theo is faced with a new burden. Palma retreats, like a frightened child, into her studio, and Theo has to spend all of his time caring for his father. His world stops. His mother wants him to leave high school, and his dream of attending MIT disappears from the future. To make things even worse, he has little time to spend with Ivy. But thoughtful and strong Ivy and some of her friends help Theo to look at himself, his responsibilities, and his needs. With "the wonder drug of Ivy's company," Theo discovers the strength to face his dilemma and chart his future. The author effectively presents the "complexities of deafness and American Sign Language." She indicates characters signing with boldface type smoothly translated into Standard English.

Subjects: art, deaf, high school, physically handicapped, sign language

53   Flake, Sharon G. *The Skin I'm In*. Hyperion. 1999. Paperback 192pp. Ages: 12 and up. ISBN: 0–7868–1307–5 $5.99.

Seventh-grader Maleeka Madison thinks she is a freak. She thinks she is the darkest, tallest, skinniest, and "worse-dressed thing in school." She is also smart and liked by her teachers. Her classmates always call her names, push, shove, and cheat off her. She tries desperately to fit into her inner-city McClenton Middle School. When a new teacher, Miss Saunders, whose face is blotched with a giant white mark, starts school, Maleeka knows that the new teacher will be taunted as well. Maleeka is right, but Miss Saunders explains that she was born with the skin condition and that in having to deal with being called a freak, she "figured she'd better love what God gave her." She explains to Maleeka that it takes a long time to accept yourself for who you are, especially if it doesn't fit anyone else's idea of beauty. Maleeka's mother gives the same advice. Nevertheless, in Maleeka's struggle to fit in and in her battle against low self-esteem that many black girls face when they are darker skinned, she becomes friends with mouthy Charlese and her tough peers. Maleeka does Charlese's homework in return for stylish clothes, gets into trouble for skipping class and smoking, and even causes a fire in Miss Saunders's classroom. But Maleeka is too bright for this. She finds comfort in writing a fictional slave girl's diary that grew out of a creative writing project assigned by Miss Saunders. She wins the affection of Caleb, one of the most popular boys in school, and eventually learns to stand up to Charlese. Maleeka is a charming, annoying, fascinating, and enlightening character in this fast-paced, lesson-filled story about acceptance.

Subjects: African Americans, facial disfiguration, middle school, self-perception, skin, teachers

54 Fleischman, Paul. *Mind's Eye*. Henry Holt & Co. 1999. Hardcover 108pp. Ages: 12 and up. ISBN: 0–8050–6314–5 $15.95.

Courtney, age sixteen, and Elva, age eighty-eight, share a room that has a broken television in Briarwood Convalescent Home in Bismarck, North Dakota. Courtney severed her spinal cord in a riding accident. Her father took off when she was two years old, and her mom remarried but died last year. Her stepfather, not wanting to take care of Courtney, placed her in the nursing home. She has no other family. Her friends don't want to visit her, which is fine because she doesn't like anyone seeing her paralyzed. Courtney will never walk again. Elva taught high school English for thirty-two years, still quotes Whittier, Milton, and Blake, is comforted by her memories of art, music, and literature, and will always be a teacher. She was married to Emmett, who died suddenly when he was fifty-eight. They always dreamed of traveling to Italy. Elva is nearly blind and lives in her mind, which "is so much more sustaining than the life of the body." She encourages Courtney to remake herself, build inner resources, and spend hours on her mind because it's there that she will run and dance and fly. She must be her own Scheherazade and keep herself alive. Courtney can do what Elva can't do—that is, read—and together they embark on an imaginary journey to Italy, with the help of a 1910 edition of Baedecker's *Italy*. Courtney is reluctant at first but soon discovers the power of the life of the mind. The complex story is written as a play script, consisting of the roommates' contrasting dialogue and simple directions for pauses. A map of Italy opens each chapter of the journey. The maps, "food for the imagination," enlarge as the play proceeds, symbolizing Courtney's growing mind's eye.

Subjects: blind, healthcare facilities, intergenerational relationships, Italy, physically handicapped, self-perception

55   Fleming, Virginia. *Be Good to Eddie Lee.* Philomel. 1993. Paperback 32pp. Ages: 4–8. ISBN: 0–698–11582–1 $5.99. Illustrated by Floyd Cooper.

It's summer vacation, and Christy's mama tells her to be good to Eddie Lee because he is so lonesome and different. Eddie Lee has Down syndrome. When Christy and her friend, Jim Bud, go wading in search of frog eggs and Eddie Lee tags along, Jim Bud tells him to go home. Eddie Lee follows them anyway and his feelings are hurt as Jim Bud continues to be mean to him. Eddie Lee runs off into the woods and Christy goes after him. He takes her to a miniature lake in the woods where he shows her frog eggs and water lilies. She wants to take the frog eggs home, but Eddie Lee, who is sensitive to nature, urges that they leave them undisturbed. The real discovery of the day, however, is that what matters is what's in the heart. The oil wash paintings of the natural world glow, and they are just soft enough to diminish the children's physical differences. The descriptive language captures the beauty of a southern summer day and the true feelings, honesty, and gentleness of this child with Down syndrome. This is a lovely picture book with a positive message.

Subjects: Down syndrome, mentally handicapped, nature

56   Fletcher, Ralph. *Flying Solo.* Yearling. 2000. Paperback 138pp. Ages: 10 and up. ISBN: 0–440–41601–9 $4.99.

On Friday, April 28, Mr. "Fab" Fabiano's sixth-grade class has a substitute teacher who doesn't show up. The children know what to do. They decide to run the day according to Mr. Fab's routine. They want to prove that kids rule, and they do surprisingly well. Smart Karen Ballard gives the class the idea in the first place and becomes the leader. Rachel White is one of the students in the sixth grade. Rachel has been silent for six months since classmate Tommy Feathers died. Psychologists diagnosed her as a selective mute: a person who chooses not to speak. This temporary condition is caused by a profound emotional trauma. Her parents are encouraged and hopeful, but they don't understand. They think her voice is lost and she will find it one day. But it isn't lost. Rachel finds it whenever she wants as soon as she picks up her pen. Rachel communicates by writing notes; because of her silence, she has learned to watch and notice things. The kid-ruled classroom runs smoothly for six hours until a fight breaks out between Bastian Fauvell and Rachel over Tommy Feathers. The kids reveal their thoughts about Tommy and come to terms with their feelings of guilt and grief. They have things to say, and so does Rachel. There is "a time to keep silence and a time to speak." Rachel knew she wouldn't keep quiet for the rest of her life. And this day becomes the right time for her to choose to speak. This quick-read is a thoughtful and comic story about an unusual school day.

Subjects: death, elective mutism, grief, middle school

57 Fletcher, Susan. *Shadow Spinner*. Atheneum. 1998. Hardcover 219pp. Ages: 9 and up. ISBN: 0–689–81852–1 $17.00.

This exciting first-person adventure offers a new twist to the tale of the fabled Shahrazad from *The Arabian Nights* who wins her life each night with interesting stories for the bloodthirsty Sultan. Young crippled Marjan loves stories and is the best storyteller in the city. Her auntie, Chava, calls her "spinning shadows" very practical. As in the case of Sharazad, "stories can save your life." Auntie Chava wonders what will become of Marjan. Marjan will always be someone else's servant. She will probably never marry, because no one would want a bride with a maimed foot. Marjan tries to hide her limp, but children stare at her and laugh. She wasn't crippled from birth. Supposedly it was an accident. But Marjan finds out later that her mother smashed her foot with a heavy pot, out of love. She maimed her to keep her safe from the Sultan. He was killing a wife every night, and because he wouldn't want an imperfect bride, Marjan's mother hurt her to protect her. Then Marjan's mother drank poison and died. However, Marjan and her storytelling talent are discovered and she is taken to live in the Sultan's harem. Shahrazad needs the "clever cripple" because she is running out of rich stories that will keep her and the remaining unmarried girls in the city alive. Marjan is forced to sneak from the harem into the dangerous streets of the bazaar, find an old storyteller who tells her the end of the Sultan's favorite boyhood story, and bring the ending back to Shahrazad. The story is an allegory, which allows the Sultan to realize his love for Shahrazad and to spare her life. Marjan then sets off for a new life where being crippled, poor, or a woman will not be an obstacle to living out dreams. Boxed "Lessons for Life and Storytelling" precede each chapter and state truths about the potential of literature. Marjan observes that being crippled doesn't necessarily mean having a crippled foot or hand. You can be crippled in your heart. She comments that "words are how the powerless can have power." And she suggests that we should freely share our stories across borders or "we will all be strangers forever." An author's note gives historical background and sources for this exotic and suspenseful re-creation of the classic tale.

Subjects: Iran, legends, physically handicapped, storytellers

58   Foland, Constance. *A Song for Jeffrey* (American Girl Fiction). Pleasant Company Publications. Paperback 179pp. Ages: 10 and up. ISBN: 1–56247–754–4 $9.95.

This story of the friendship of two eleven-year-olds is part of the American Girl series. Dodie is bored and lonely, and her parents have separated. Jeffrey is new to the neighborhood. He has muscular dystrophy and uses a wheelchair. Dodie is curious at first but really wants to be his friend. Her persistence wears down his resistance, and they become close friends. Dodie loves to sing, and Jeffrey loves to paint and draw. Their talents unite them even more. They enter a talent show at Jeffrey's clinic. Their performance about friendship features an original song by Dodie and a mural painted by Jeffrey. However, Jeffrey's health deteriorates rapidly, he is hospitalized, and Dodie has to perform alone. Dodie faces up to the reality of Jeffrey's disease and recognizes her own good fortune in having Jeffrey as a good friend. This book doesn't hide certain tough issues, as it gives truthful answers to Dodie's questions about being physically challenged by muscular dystrophy.

Subjects: art, healthcare facilities, muscular dystrophy, music, physically handicapped, wheelchairs

59   Foreman, Michael. *Seal Surfer*. Harcourt Brace Children's Books. 1997. Hardcover 36pp. Ages: 5–10. ISBN: 0–15–201399–7 $16.00. Illustrated by the author.

Although Ben's disability is never mentioned in the text, the illustrations show that he uses a wheelchair or crutches to get around. Much of this touching story's interest can be found in the watercolor pictures, which are dramatic, expansive, and colored in the intense blues and greens of the sea. One day, while fishing with his grandfather, Ben witnesses the birth of a seal pup. Ben and the pup learn to play together in the surf, where Ben moves around easily on a surfboard fastened to his wrist. Many events take place over the course of three years. Ben and his father feed fish to the seal while listening to Beethoven; Ben is rescued by the seal after being flipped from his board by a huge rolling wave. The third summer, Ben returns to the cliffs with his friends but not his grandfather; Ben rides the waves with the seal that summer and every summer and finally contemplates the day he might return to the cliff tops with his own grandchildren to watch the seals. The sensitive portrait of a disabled boy, his relationship with his grandfather, and the extraordinary bond between the young boy and the seal make this a valuable book for all generations.

Subjects: England, grandparents, intergenerational relationships, nature, physically handicapped, sports, swimming, wheelchairs

60   Fraustino, Lisa Rowe. *The Hickory Chair*. Arthur A. Levine Books/Scholastic. 2001. Hardcover 32pp. Ages: 4–8. ISBN: 0–590–52248–5 $15.95. Illustrated by Benny Andrews.

Louis has been blind since birth, so he has what his Gran calls "blind sight," because of his ability to "see" so much. He knows Gran because of her rich molasses voice, her alive smell of lilacs and bleach, her warm face, and her salty kisses. He and Gran sit in her favorite chair, which Grandpa carved from hickory, and read and tell each other stories. Gran is good at hide-and-seek and especially at hiding surprise notes for her family members. After her death they find that she has devised a family treasure hunt as a part of her will. She left notes for each of the family member children in one of her favorite things telling them what they were to keep for themselves. Louis finds everyone's note but his. Could she have overlooked him? Years later, when Louis is a grandfather, his grandchild discovers the note in Gran's much-loved hickory chair. His faith in Gran is affirmed. What is important cannot be seen. The sensuous text and the bright oil and fabric collage artwork reveal the textures of Louis's world. A note acknowledges the National Braille Press for its help and advice on the book.

Subjects: African Americans, blind, grandparents, intergenerational relationships, physically handicapped

61   Furlong, Monica. *Robin's Country*. Knopf. 1995. Paperback 139pp. Ages: 10 and up. ISBN: 0–679–89099–8 $4.99.

In this retelling of the age-old Robin Hood legend, ten-year-old Dummy, who is mute and has no memory of his childhood, escapes from a cruel master and finds himself in Robin Hood's secret hideaway deep in Sherwood Forest. At first he is afraid of outlaws, and they suspect he is a spy for the evil Prince John. He struggles to speak, but because communication is difficult, he can't defend himself. Eventually they learn to trust each other, and Dummy becomes one of Robin's men. Robin is actually kind and brave, and Dummy appreciates Robin's trickery and recklessness. And because Marian is the best archer, she teaches Dummy how to shoot a bow. A second plot involves Dummy's discovery of his true identity, which is hinted at very early in the story, and the recovery of his voice. In the end, King Richard returns and recognizes Dummy as his godson. The book is filled with adventure, courage, honor, and humor that are accessible to intermediate readers.

Subjects: elective mutism, England, legends

62   Gantos, Jack. *Joey Pigza Loses Control*. Farrar, Straus & Giroux. 2000. Hardcover 196pp. Ages: 9–12. ISBN: 0–374–39989–1 $16.00.

In this continuation of the Joey Pigza story, Joey is on a summer visit with his self-destructive and alcoholic father who skipped out when Joey was in kindergarten. With the help of his new continuous-release medicine patches, Joey is in charge of his attention-deficit disorder. The problem is that Joey's dad, Carter, is as wired as Joey used to be. Carter claims to have turned over a new leaf, and at first he is high-spirited and fun. He takes Joey to Storybook Land, where he uses Humpty Dumpty, the Old Lady Who Lives in a Shoe, and others to explain his philosophies of life and of coaching Little League baseball. He wants to teach Joey how to be a winner. Joey is very optimistic about his father and yearns for his love and attention. When Joey becomes the star pitcher on his dad's team, he feels extreme pressure to be the winner his dad wants him to be. Carter decides Joey can take control of his life and be a normal kid without medication. He flushes the patches down the toilet and leaves Joey on his own in downtown Pittsburgh. Joey is torn between wanting to call his mom right away and toughing it out with his father. He wants his dad to be right, but Carter becomes increasingly irresponsible, domineering, and frightening. Joey, off his meds and scared as his old behavior returns, agitates Carter into a wild rage. Joey finally calls his mom to rescue him. The mood of this story is more thoughtful and less breathless than it is in *Joey Pigza Swallowed the Key* because Joey himself isn't so hyperactive. Joey really struggles to keep control, and he grows to understand himself and his family. Joey's first-person narrative is both sad and comical. His courage and genuine goodness make him a great kid.

Subjects: attention-deficit hyperactivity disorder, baseball, learning disabled, sports

63   Gantos, Jack. *Joey Pigza Swallowed the Key*. Farrar, Straus & Giroux. 1998. Hardcover 154pp. Ages: 9–12. ISBN: 0–374–33664–4 $16.00.

Being hyperactive runs in Joey's family. Joey's alcoholic father ran off when Joey was in kindergarten, and his mother, who also drinks, left shortly afterwards. He's been in the care of his nutty and abusive grandmother. For years, Joey's teachers blamed his bad behavior on his hyperactive grandmother. His mom returns, sobered up and determined to start over. Joey is on medication, but it only works half a day, and then Joey can't sit still. He is so wired that he bounces off the walls and is a danger to himself and his classmates. He disrupts a field trip, swallows his house key (and brings it up again), hurts his finger in the pencil sharpener, and accidentally injures a classmate when he runs with scissors. He doesn't mean to get into trouble. He just can't help himself. Because he is impossible in his regular classroom, he is sent to special education classes and then to a special education school. There, he encounters a caring teacher, Special Ed. Through counseling, positive reinforcement, and a continuous-release patch that evens out the delivery of his drugs, Joey calms down and is allowed to return to his former school. The story is written from Joey's point of view in a worried and breathless style that swerves out of control when Joey does. It is both funny and sad. Because it shows ADHD from the inside, it is enlightening for teachers and parents. Joey provides the key to the world of a hyperactive child.

Subjects: attention-deficit hyperactivity disorder, grandparents, learning disabled, special education, teachers

64 Garland, Sherry. *The Silent Storm*. Harcourt Brace Jovanovich. 1993. Hardcover 240pp. Ages: 9–12. ISBN: 0–15–274170–4 $14.95.

Thirteen-year-old Alyssa MacAllister has been unable to speak since witnessing her mother drown and her father vanish in a hurricane three years ago. When she opens her mouth, her throat grows tight, and fearful memories rush toward her. At school she is in a special education class and her friends reject her. They call her "crazy" or "mental case" or "Looney Tunes." She hates the tests the nurses and psychiatrists give her to find out why she can't speak and agrees with the doctors that if she could just remember what happened on the charter boat the day it sank, she would be able to speak again. She believes that the accident that day was in some way her fault. Alyssa lives with her grandfather on Galveston Island, Texas, and loves her green boat and her grandfather's mustang horses, especially Stormy, her favorite. When another hurricane approaches, "the memory monster inside her" tries to get free. Flashbacks come faster and faster. The hurricane hits, and Alyssa is trapped on a shrimp boat headed toward Louisiana. She is desperate to get back to her grandfather and his horses. By the time she gets home, her grandfather has been seriously injured. In the hospital, delirious, he mumbles about Alyssa being dead because of him. She knows that if she can tell him she's alive, he might gain the extra strength he needs to survive. The "memory monster" awakens, and scenes of the first hurricane flash into her mind. She remembers her father putting her in the lifeboat, saying he would return with her mother. She also remembers the promise she made to her father to be brave and not to cry or say a word until he joined her. For three years she keeps the promise, believing her father will return if she doesn't speak. Facing her fears and reliving the tragedy finally enable her to speak. She breaks her promise and in doing so saves her grandfather. Vivid language and drama enhance this compelling adventure about a spunky teen who faces the silent storm within her that causes her inability to speak.

Subjects: elective mutism, grandparents, intergenerational relationships, middle school, special education

65 Gifaldi, David. *Ben, King of the River*. Albert Whitman & Co. 2001. Hardcover 32pp. Ages: 4–8. ISBN: 0–8075–0635–4 $14.95. Illustrated by Layne Johnson.

Chad can't wait for his first family camping trip. He just hopes that Ben doesn't ruin it. Ben is Chad's five-year-old developmentally disabled brother. He wears diapers, has allergies, and doesn't like new things. He loves sing-along videos and can run a VCR as well as anyone else. At the campground Chad thinks Ben is a baby because Ben screams when a bug flies around his head. When the family goes swimming Ben runs into the water with his arms raised high like he is King of the River. He's not afraid, but Chad keeps a close eye on him anyway. While they are swimming, two boys make fun of Ben. It doesn't bother Ben, but it annoys Chad. Later that night the four boys meet on a trail and when Ben greets them as if he's known them all his life, Chad explains that Ben likes to hug people. The story shows that it's not easy for siblings of children with disabilities. Chad's frustration, embarrassment, shame, patience, and understanding are conveyed in the narration and the expressive watercolor illustrations. Chad's life is more complicated because of his brother, but it can also be more rewarding. A note by the thirteen-year-old nephew of the author describes what it's like living with a disabled sibling, and a list of tips is included for children who live with a disabled brother or sister.

Subjects: mentally handicapped, nature, siblings

66 Giff, Patricia Reilly. *All the Way Home*. Delacorte Press. 2001. Hardcover 169pp. Ages: 9–12: ISBN: 0–385–32209–7 $15.95.

Preteens Mariel Manning and Brick Tiernan meet in Brooklyn in August 1941. Mariel was hospitalized at the age of four with polio and taken care of by Loretta, a nurse who subsequently adopted her. Now they live near Ebbets Field and are Dodgers fans. Mariel doesn't know what happened to her birth mother, but she is determined to find out. She is self-conscious when kids at school look at her polio-scarred legs, which to her are "curved like the pretzels in Jordan's candy store." She wears overalls to hide her legs and reminds everyone that President Roosevelt can't walk because of polio. He never gave up and now he's one of the greatest presidents. Brick is in Brooklyn because a fire destroyed his family's apple orchard and his parents had to leave the farm to find work elsewhere. He is sent to live temporarily with their friend Loretta, but he wants to return to Windy Hill in upstate New York to save what's left of the apple harvest. The excitement of attending a Dodgers game is the only good thing he can say about Brooklyn. But Brick and Mariel become close friends, and together they run off to Windy Hill to save the apples and to visit the hospital where Mariel spent two years. Brick is invited to stay in Windy Hill with elderly neighbors, and Mariel finds out the truth about her mother. Rich period details add interest to this work of historical fiction about friendship, determination, and a strong-willed girl who, like FDR, doesn't let her disability keep her from winning.

Subjects: adoption, baseball, Brooklyn, historical fiction, physically handicapped, poliomyelitis, self-perception, sports

67 Gillmore, Rachna. *A Screaming Kind of Day.* Fitzhenry & Whiteside. 1999. Hardcover 32pp. Ages: 4–8. ISBN: 1–55041–514–X $15.95. Illustrated by Gordon Sauve.

Scully, a young girl who is hearing impaired, wants to play outside in the rain, but because she and her brother have been fighting all morning they have been sent to their rooms. Determined, Scully sneaks out anyway to dance with the rain, shout with the green, and catch the "whoosh" of the rain. She flops to the ground so her arms can "listen to the rain shaking the earth." This makes her mom mad, and Scully is grounded for the rest of the day. In the end, harmony is restored and Scully, her mom, and her brother share a special moment outside watching the stars come out. Scully turns her hearing aids off to listen to the stars sing. Vivid imagery in the text reveals how important nature is to Scully. "The pink sky melts into red and then blue." "The green smells full and glad." At the same time, the text provides insight into Scully's personality. She behaves like any child her age, but she also uses the convenience of turning off or removing her hearing aids to help her get her way. The illustrations are realistic, and the variety of vantage points enriches the beauty of the story.

Subjects: deaf, nature, physically handicapped

68   Goldin, Barbara Diamond. *Cakes and Miracles: A Purim Tale*. Viking. 1991. Hardcover 32pp. Ages: 5–8. ISBN: 0–670–83047–X. Out of print. Illustrated by Erika Weins.

Young Hershel is blind, but that doesn't stop him from playing in the mud by the river or misbehaving in school. However, it does stop him from helping his hard-working mother prepare the three-cornered fat cakes called hamantashen for the Jewish holiday of Purim. He goes to bed and dreams about an angel who tells him he can help by making what he sees in his head. The next day he begs his mother to let him make cookies in wonderful shapes, but she is afraid he will just ruin the dough. That night, he can't sleep and is drawn to the kitchen. He feels the bowl filled with dough, kneads the dough, and shapes cookies into birds, fish, and other images he sees dancing in his head. In the morning his mother is amazed by his delicious cookie creations. They take his Purim treats to the marketplace, where all the townspeople buy them. Hershel can't see the excitement, but he feels it all around him. The joy of the holiday is described in the text and in an author's note about Purim. A recipe for hamantashen is included. The warm, rich paintings celebrate the light and gladness of Hershel's story.

Subjects: blind, physically handicapped, religion

69   Gregory, Nan. *How Smudge Came*. Red Deer College Press. 1995. Hardcover 32pp. Ages: 5–8. ISBN: 0–88995–143–8 $15.95. Illustrated by Ron Lightburn.

Cindy, a young woman with Down syndrome, lives in a group home and has a cleaning job at Hospice House. She finds a stray puppy in the rain and hides it in her room because dogs are not allowed where she lives. Cindy knows the puppy is her best friend. She also knows to concentrate on her work, "think about the plates, not the puppy." She puts the puppy in the pocket of her apron while she cleans. Jan, a hospice patient who is nearly blind, hears the puppy whimper, and when Cindy places it on Jan's bed, Jan names the puppy Smudge because he can only see the black puppy as a smudge in the dark. But rules are rules, and Cindy has to give up the puppy. She cries when Smudge is taken to the SPCA. She is also furious and knows how to get around. With the address of the SPCA and her bus pass, she goes to the animal shelter, finds Smudge in a cage, and is told that she can have her puppy back if she returns on Saturday. She does this only to discover that Smudge is gone. For Cindy, there's no place to go now but home. She lies on her bed, humming, until she gets a call to go to Hospice House. There, everyone is waiting for her, including Smudge. Cindy knows that this is the perfect place for a puppy. This quiet story is told from Cindy's viewpoint. Her disability is not mentioned in the text, but it is revealed in the soft, colored pencil drawings, in her direct, clipped speech, and in how she processes her daily activities. Cindy is strong-willed and caring and has helpful and understanding friends.

Subjects: blind, dogs, Down syndrome, healthcare facilities, mentally handicapped

70 Harrar, George. *Parents Wanted*. Milkweed Editions. 2001. Paperback 239pp. Ages: 12 and up. ISBN: 1–57131–633–7 $6.95. Illustrated by Dan Murphy.

Twelve-year-old Andy Fleck, who describes himself as obnoxious, has already been in eight foster homes. He has attention-deficit hyperactivity disorder and is on Ritalin and Depakote for it. His alcoholic mother gave him up to the state because she couldn't handle him, and his father is in and out of jail for stealing. Andy desperately wants to be adopted by a normal family, but his own stealing, lying, anger, getting into trouble at school, and desire to break things, like windows, keep families from wanting him. One day he meets Laurie and Jeff at an adoption party, and they do want him. He likes living with them. He gets pancakes on Sundays and his own TV. Still, he challenges every limit they set. Andy has a tough decision to make when his "first" dad shows up and asks Andy to steal money from Jeff, his "last" dad. Finally, Andy gets sent back to the Brighton Boys Home, when he falsely accuses Jeff of inappropriate touching. But Laurie and Jeff don't give up on him, and Andy discovers what he has to do if he wants a real family. Mutual trust develops, and Laurie and Jeff officially adopt him. Andy adopts them, too, figuring that since his first mom and dad didn't want him as their kid, he should be free to get other parents. For a time after everything is official, he behaves perfectly. But when his yo-yo accidentally breaks a mirror, he realizes that now he can get into trouble, like any other kid, and still have a family. Andy is authentically portrayed as an adopted ADHD preteen with a strong need for acceptance.

Subjects: adoption, attention-deficit hyperactivity disorder, learning disabled

71 Harshman, Marc. *The Storm*. Dutton Children's Books. 1995. Hardcover 32pp. Ages: 5–8. ISBN: 0–5256–5150–0 $15.99. Illustrated by Mark Mohr.

Jonathan, a gradeschooler who uses a wheelchair, hates the way his classmates single him out as the one who is afraid of storms and always needs help. He is not afraid of storms. He loves them, especially when he and his dad watch the lightning flash darkness into daylight. And he doesn't always need special help. He and his therapists work hard to make the rest of his body as strong as possible. There are ramps in his house and low rope handles on the barn doors, so Jonathan is very capable around his family's Indiana farm. When a tornado tears a path of ruin through the farm, Jonathan's swift action saves his father's prize horses. Although the text is a bit long, it is a dramatic account of the raging storm and a strong-willed child with a disability who can take care of himself and the horses. Uneven impressionistic watercolor paintings using electric colors convey a powerful tornado experience.

Subjects: elementary school, horses, physically handicapped, wheelchairs

72 Helfman, Elizabeth. *On Being Sarah*. Albert Whitman & Co. 1993. Hardcover 173pp. Ages: 9–12. ISBN: 0–8075–6068–5 $13.95. Illustrated by Lino Saffioti.

The title of the first chapter, "Talk to Me, Not about Me!" says it all in this successful novel about twelve-year-old Sarah who has cerebral palsy. She uses a motorized wheelchair to move independently and Blissymbols to communicate. She is mainstreamed into a regular school; becomes best friends with Maggie, who learns to read Sarah's symbols; and meets a boy who also cannot walk but shows her new worlds. Like most girls, she wants to be recognized as an individual and dreams of her future. Sarah is complex, introspective, and determined. Her family is made up of her loving but jealous sister, her all-giving mother, and her father, who hasn't come to terms with his daughter's cerebral palsy. Together, Sarah's family and friends help her grow and meet the special challenges of her disability. An afterword tells about Charles Bliss and his system of symbols for people who use alternatives to oral speech. Blissymbols are integrated throughout the story.

Subjects: Blissymbols, cerebral palsy, middle school, siblings, wheelchairs

73 Hermann, Spring. *Seeing Lessons: The Story of Abigail Carter and America's First School for Blind People.* Henry Holt & Co. 1998. Hardcover 176pp. Ages: 9–12. ISBN: 0–8050–5706–4 $15.95. Illustrated by Ib Ohlsson.

In America in the 1820s, no schools for the blind existed. It was believed that blind children should stay home with their families. While studying in Paris, John Fisher, a Boston medical student, discovered the National Institution for Blind Youth. There he saw blind teachers and blind children reading books, writing stories, doing math, playing music, and creating art. He and Dr. Samuel Gridley Howe opened such a school in Boston with two blind teachers who came from Scotland and France to teach in the school. Ten-year-old Abigail Carter and her six-year-old sister, Sophia, became the first students in the Perkins School for the Blind, the first school for blind people in America. This fictionalized account of the school uses information from letters, journals, school reports, memoirs, and articles to tell Abby's story. Abby and Sophia, both blind since birth, start out, in 1932, in a large house owned by Dr. Howe with four other blind children and their teachers, determined to prove that blind people can learn as well as anyone else. They read raised print books—*English Stories* and the Gospel of John from the Bible—and Abby describes the thrill racing through her fingertips to her heart. They have music lessons and discover they have special talents for playing the piano. And for geography, they use a raised map of Massachusetts made of twine and glue. The lessons are hard to learn, but they get to be "like breathing." "The words of someone long ago or far away (travel) from books to (Abby's) fingers and into (her) head. That (is) reading!" The same occurs with writing and making music. They are "seeing lessons." All the students learn to read, write, play, and sing. They discover that they have choices and that blind people can dream and do just about anything. But the school has financial problems. Finally the school receives six thousand dollars when the students demonstrate to the legislators at the statehouse that the blind can learn as well as common school pupils can. An afterword explains that both Abby and Sophia grew up to be musicians and teachers at the Perkins Institution, which also graduated Annie Sullivan, Helen Keller's teacher.

Subjects: blind, books and reading, Boston, historical fiction, music, physically handicapped, siblings, special education

74 Hesser, Terry Spencer. *Kissing Doorknobs.* Bantam Books. 1998. Paperback 149pp. Ages: 12 and up. ISBN: 0–440–41314–1 $4.99.

Middle-schooler Tara Sullivan is ruled by the "tyrants in her head." She has lost possession of her thoughts, is driven by irrational fears, and is compelled to perform peculiar behaviors she can't control. She counts sidewalk cracks on her way to school, incessantly recites prayers, lines up food on her plate, touches doorknobs with all ten fingers, and then kisses her fingers thirty-three times before leaving the house. She gets no pleasures from her odd quirks and recognizes them as absurd behavior, yet she is enslaved by her habits. She can't stop. Her neighbors are puzzled, her friends become frustrated and alienated, her mother drinks and reacts with violence, and her parents fight about everything. For years, her condition is misdiagnosed as attention-deficit disorder, immaturity, borderline anorexia, and anger issues. Finally a concerned teacher recognizes her doorknob kissing ritual as a symptom of obsessive-compulsive disorder (OCD). Tara also meets Sam, a fellow sufferer, and discovers that she is not alone. OCD affects about 1 out of 100 children and adolescents. Tara begins behavior therapy, and there is hope that she will regain control of her life. This realistic story not only explores the pain, isolation, humiliation, and fear experienced by Tara, but also the anxiety and agony of her parents and sibling. The account is honest and intense, yet sprinkled with humor. It shows that people can live with OCD and recover from it. An afterword answers questions about the causes of and treatments for this mysterious disorder and suggests sources of information on OCD and related conditions.

Subjects: emotional problems, mentally ill, middle school, obsessive-compulsive disorder

75 Hill, David. *See Ya, Simon*. Dutton Children's Books. 1996. Hardcover 153pp. Ages: 12 and up. ISBN: 0–525–45247–8 $14.99.

Confined to a wheelchair because of muscular dystrophy, fourteen-year-old Simon is "bad-tempered and funny" and "fierce-tongued and brave." He has a passion for soccer, computers, and girls. Nathan, Simon's best friend, narrates this keenly sensitive story about their relationship. Simon is a complex character who is intelligent, strongly opinionated, and adjusted to his situation. He lashes out against telethons that treat the disabled like outsiders. They want to be treated like other kids as much as possible. "All the Spina Bifida kids and MD kids and cerebral palsy kids . . . want to live like—live with—able-bodied kids as much as they can . . . we don't want your bloody pity, we want your world!" Nathan provides an eye-opening look at Simon's world, as Simon grows steadily weaker. Nathan is a perspicacious teen. He is frightened and angry about losing someone so important to him. He also feels lucky, yet guilty, because he drew an easier lot. Although Simon dies in the end, Nathan knows that the world is "full of good things that could happen." Life goes on, "without Simon, but with all sorts of memories of him." Set in New Zealand, this poignant novel gives a wealth of information about muscular dystrophy. A Reading for Real Teacher's Guide to *See Ya, Simon* is available from the Developmental Studies Center. 2000 Embarcadero, Suite 305, Oakland, CA 94606–5300.

Subjects: death, middle school, muscular dystrophy, New Zealand, physically handicapped, wheelchairs

76 Hill, Elizabeth Starr. *Bird Boy.* Farrar, Straus & Giroux. 1999. Hardcover 64pp. Ages: 9–12. ISBN: 0–374–30723–7 $15.00. Illustrated by Leslie Lui.

Young Chang cannot speak, but he has a special relationship with the cormorants his father uses for fishing and can imitate their sounds. He lives with his parents on a houseboat on the Li River in China. Chang's father decides that Chang is old enough to raise a cormorant chick and go along on the year's major fishing trip, when thousands of fish gather in a particular spot on the river. Chang loves the birds and is thrilled, but soon he discovers that it is quite a challenge. The neighborhood bully, Jinan, steals his cormorant chick, and Chang has to rescue the bird and nurse it back to health. He proves himself and also learns a lesson about trust and friendship. The Taiwanese illustrator's enthralling drawings capture the southern Chinese landscape and promote a vivid awareness of this fascinating part of the world.

Subjects: birds, bullies, China, mutism

77 Hill, Kirkpatrick. *The Year of Miss Agnes.* McElderry/Simon & Schuster. 2000. Hardcover 128pp. Ages: 8–12. ISBN: 0–689–82933–7 $16.00.

It's 1948, and Miss Agnes Sutterfield is the new teacher in the one-room schoolhouse of a small Athabascan village on the Koyukuk River in Alaska. Ten-year-old Fredericka (Fred) and her classmates find Miss Agnes to be "different, but good different." Miss Agnes wears pants instead of dresses, reads *Robin Hood* and Greek myths, plays opera recordings, puts their desks in a circle, and doesn't hate the smell of fish. Fred's twelve-year-old sister, Bokko, is deaf and doesn't go to school. Their old teacher didn't know how to teach deaf children. And their Mamma said Bokko didn't need school anyway because she could stay home and learn to cook and sew. But Miss Agnes is different. She convinces Mamma to let Bokko attend school, where she has special sign language books. Miss Agnes explains about sign language and lip-reading and that there is even a way that blind people can read. Bokko learns over 200 signs, and everyone in the school learns sign language, too. A lot of the grown-ups in the village and even Mamma learn to sign. Miss Agnes has her students do a lot of different things that are fun. She connects her teaching to Athabascan culture. The children sing songs and dance. Bokko touches the concertina so she can feel the music. At Christmastime they have a tree in the school and put on "A Christmas Carol." And best of all, Miss Agnes tells her students what they are good at and encourages them to become scientists and doctors. This is a warm story about Alaska and a dedicated teacher who "opens a door to the world" for all of her students, especially Fred and her deaf sister, Bokko.

Subjects: Alaska, deaf, historical fiction, music, Native Americans, physically handicapped, sign language, teachers

78 Hobbs, Valerie. *Carolina Crow Girl*. Farrar, Straus & Giroux. 1999. Hardcover 138pp. Ages: 9–12. ISBN: 0–374–31153–6 $16.00.

Eleven-year-old Carolina lives with her mother, Melanie, and her little sister, Trinity, in an old yellow school bus. They are always moving. They stop wherever Melanie can find work. Carolina longs to live in a real house, but the wheels make them free to follow Red, who is Trinity's father but not Carolina's, wherever he goes. This time, they stop in a field adjacent to the mansion home of wheelchair-bound Stefan Crouch and his overprotective mother. Stefan's wheels do not make him free. In the field, Carolina rescues a baby crow and decides to keep and protect him until he can fly. She befriends Stefan, who has a keen interest in the natural world, and who is a loner like she is. Stefan's socialite mother takes an interest in Carolina as a surrogate for her own daughter who died four years ago after a fall from a horse. When Melanie decides to follow Red to Oregon, Carolina and Crow stay behind to live with Stefan's family. Carolina soon realizes that her place is with Melanie and Trinity, no matter how poor and imperfect they are. Stefan's mother, surprisingly, does not try to suffocate Carolina. Because she understands emotional loss, she helps Carolina to return to live in the old yellow school bus with her real family. Carolina also discovers that keeping Crow is wrong. So she lets him fly free. Both Carolina and Stefan are especially strong characters. They, too, learn to fly free. This novel, filled with symbolism, explores ideas of socioeconomic status, stability, change, and freedom.

Subjects: birds, nature, physically handicapped, wheelchairs

79 Holt, Kimberly Willis. *When Zachary Beaver Came to Town*. Henry Holt & Co. 1999. Hardcover 227pp. Ages: 9 and up. ISBN: 0–8050–6116–9 $16.95.

It's summer 1971 in Antler, Texas, where nothing ever happens, until a Christmas-light-decorated trailer arrives carrying Zachary Beaver, the world's fattest boy. Zachary is mean, angry, unfriendly, and a misfit and a liar. His obesity is a source of humor throughout the story. His personality is a reaction to the way he is treated by others. But Zachary's size is not the main issue of the book. It is Toby Wilson's coming of age. Thirteen-year-old Toby is having the most difficult summer of his life. His mother has left him and his father to become a country singer in Nashville. Scarlett, the girl of his dreams, is interested in someone else. And his best friend Cal's brother is killed in Vietnam. Toby comes to realize that others have it worse than he does. By reaching out to Zachary, bringing him food, taking him to the drive-in theatre, and finally fulfilling Zachary's dream of being baptized, Toby learns that the best way to deal with his own problems is to help others with theirs. Toby is a believable narrator. His thoughts and sentiments are true to life. The rural Texas setting and early 1970s time frame are masterfully created by descriptive writing in this novel that delivers a persuasive message of tolerance.

Subjects: historical fiction, overweight, Texas

80 Howe, James. *The Misfits*. Atheneum. 2001. Hardcover 274pp. Ages: 10 and up. ISBN: 0–689–83955–3 $16.00.

This book is about adolescents who are on the outside and who don't fit in. The four seventh graders who make up the Gang of Five, even though there are only four of them, are the misfits. The have been called seventy names altogether, such as fatso, dweeb, Einstein, greaseball, and nerd. Quirky Bobby Goodspeed narrates the story, is fat by his own admission, and never raises his hand in class for fear of being laughed at. Addie Carle is too tall and intelligent, both of which are not good traits for a twelve-year-old girl. Skeezie Tookis plays at being a 1950s hoodlum, though he's a good guy and never gets into trouble. And Joe Bunch is too creative, girlish, and openly gay. The four have always been friends, and once a week they meet at the Candy Kitchen to eat ice cream and discuss important issues. They do not feel sorry for themselves. Though other people call them names, in their own eyes the Gang of Five is okay. At school, Addie refuses to say the Pledge of Allegiance because she does not believe that there is liberty and justice for all in this country. She consequently decides to create a new political party to run for student council. The four come up with the Freedom Party, which will be a voice for minority students. When this party isn't allowed, they form the No-Name Party, which is dedicated to ending name-calling in Paintbrush Falls Middle School in upstate New York. Their slogan is "sticks and stones may break our bones, but names will break our spirit." In the process, they really shake up the school. They don't win the election, but they really are winners. They not only learn about politics, but they learn that they are brave and strong enough to be themselves, no matter what names they are called. Bobby's articulate narrative alternates with transcripts of the Candy Kitchen meetings in this coming-of-age novel about the freedom to be who you are, name-calling, and the effort to stop it.

Subjects: African Americans, middle school, overweight, popularity, self-perception

81 Hulme, Joy N. *Through the Open Door.* Harper Collins. 2000. Hardcover 176pp. Ages: 8–12. ISBN: 0–380–97870–9 $14.95.

Nine-year-old Dora Cookson has been kept out of school because she can't speak. She can't share the wonderful things she knows, and she can't ask questions. Her friends tease her and call her dumb Dora. They interpret her silence as stupidity. Dora and her family are devout Latter Day Saints living in Salt Lake City, Utah, in 1910, who are moving to a homestead near Clovis, New Mexico, where they will have more land near other Mormons. Shortly before their departure, a doctor discovers the reason Dora can't talk. She is tongue-tied, meaning that her tongue is attached to the bottom of her mouth. He performs a simple operation to correct the defect. A map is included that details the family's wagon train journey. There are plenty of adventures, including changing landscapes, desert mirages, a peaceful encounter with Navajos, and a new baby born along the way. When they get to New Mexico, it is not what they expected. The house needs a lot of work, and they have difficulty finding water. But this is more than a journey to a new home. It is a journey where Dora finds a new voice. She carefully and slowly teaches herself to speak. Though she experiences the setback of a nervous stutter, her brother and her father provide help and encouragement. She becomes a speaking member of her community. She makes new friends, tells secrets, asks questions, and fulfills her greatest dream of walking through the open schoolhouse door. This work of historical fiction is based on the true experience of a Mormon girl who grew up on a homestead in New Mexico in the early 1900s. Although it is the voice of an adult recollecting, Dora's first-person narration is a compelling account of pioneer life and of a young girl's struggle with and triumph over a speech disorder.

Subjects: historical fiction, Native Americans, New Mexico, physically handicapped, religion, speech disorders

82 Ingold, Jeanette. *The Window*. Harcourt Brace & Co. 1996. Hardcover 181pp. Ages: 12 and up. ISBN: 0–15–201265–6 $12.00.

Mandy, age fifteen, survives the car accident that killed her mother, but she is blinded. She goes to Texas to live with her great aunt and uncles, relatives who didn't know of her existence. She decides to attend the local high school instead of the special school for the blind. Mandy knows that in a school with 1,500 normal kids, they will whisper, watch, and laugh. But she's always been able to handle being the outsider, and she knows she has to take the chance because she doesn't want to disappear into the special school for blind kids. She's not about to give up and disappear from her old life. At school she makes friends with Hannah, who has been assigned to guide her around the building. Hannah won't put up with any self-pity from Mandy and pulls her into normal social life. Mandy also meets Ted, who is deaf. He greets her with "welcome to the land of the blind, deaf, lame, maimed, outraged, and outrageous." He discovers that "there's a questioning brain behind those sightless eyes" and becomes more than a friend to Mandy. When Mandy asks Ted to a dance, he responds with "so everyone can watch the blind girl being led around by the deaf boy who can't hear the music." But he's laughing a friendly laugh as he says it. At the dance, the DJ has the volume up loud enough to feel the vibrations of the music and they dance wonderfully. Mandy adjusts well to her new school and a new way of learning. Descriptions of a Braille lesson and of orientation and mobility classes are authentic and accurate. But there's more to the story. Mandy seems to hear voices and "see" things from the past, through the windows of her attic room. These visits to another time enable her to piece together her mysterious family history. Mandy has a persistent, independent voice. She suddenly has to face the world with no sight, but as Hannah says, whatever happens, Mandy charges forward and deals with it. The author learned the basics of reading Braille and found out about orientation and mobility skills so that she could experience how Mandy makes her way in a world that is experienced through senses other than sight. The author also acknowledges the Montana School for the Deaf and Blind.

Subjects: blind, Braille, deaf, fantasy, high school, physically handicapped

83   Janover, Caroline. *How Many Days until Tomorrow?* Woodbine House. 2000. Paperback 173pp. Ages: 8–12. ISBN: 1–890627–22–4 $11.95. Illustrated by Charlotte Fremaux.

This engaging novel is a sequel to *Josh: A Boy with Dyslexia* (Waterfront, 1988) and a companion to *Zipper, the Kid with ADHD* (Woodbine, 1997), both by Janover. Josh is twelve years old, dyslexic, and about to enter middle school. He and Simon, his perfect thirteen-year-old gifted and talented brother, are sent to remote Seal Island, off the coast of Maine, to spend a month at their grandparents' summer house. Gramps (Grumps) is cold and disapproves of whatever Josh does. Bookish Simon, to whom Josh is always compared, also gives Josh a hard time. Josh plots to run away but stays because his grandmother gives him love and support and because island life and the rare sea animals fascinate him. On the island, Simon reads sixteen books. Josh doesn't finish his required sixth-grade reading assignment, but he does read some chapters in the *Maine Coast Marine Life* book. Simon carefully builds a perfect model of a battleship. Josh doesn't bother with the directions for his, gives up, but eventually builds a castle out of pebbles, seashells, beach glass, sticks, and tree bark for his pet mouse. He's better at thinking up his own creations. Josh especially looks forward to when his grandmother reads *Treasure Island* by candlelight every night after dinner. When she reads aloud he can remember every detail, not like in school when he'd forget everything. Josh struggles with his disability, grows a lot, copes with his brother, and becomes a hero when he rescues his grandfather, who falls on the drain tide dock. Josh's dyslexia is really secondary to the story. His pet crabs are named Orton and Gillingham after a phonics program, and he sometimes mixes up syllables in words. More important, the story is about a dyslexic child outside the classroom who overcomes his frustration and loneliness, meets challenges, earns his grandfather's respect, and becomes devoted to the environment. Josh uses his many talents, and in the end Gramps tells him that with his "level head, cleverness, work ethic, and sensitivity to people," he will go as far in life as his studious brother will. Ten black-and-white illustrations add realism to Josh's adventure.

Subjects: books and reading, dyslexia, gifted and talented, grandparents, intergenerational relationships, learning disabled, Maine, nature, siblings

84   Janover, Caroline. *The Worst Speller in Jr. High.* Free Spirit Publishing. 1995. Paperback 200pp. Ages: 10 and up. ISBN: 0–915793–76–8 $4.95.

On the first day of seventh grade Katie Kelso promises herself that she will become a P.K., or Popular Kid, and that she will "begin dating boys by

Thanksgiving, or by Christmas vacation at the latest." Katie is dyslexic. She reads slowly, mixes up letters, forgets numbers, gets "a little lost" at school, and is "probly the worst speller in 7th grade." Katie is a bright girl. She enjoys art and writing, and her English teacher tells her that she writes "with creative flair." She works hard in school and understands that being dyslexic means that she thinks a little differently. Katie goes to the Learning Center for extra support, and she has a tutor. She knows learning strategies, like underlining main ideas and drawing time lines and pictures to facilitate remembering the sequence of the plot, that she needs to succeed. Katie confronts typical teen issues. Good-looking but trouble-making Spud Larson seems to like her. So does Brian Straus, who is smart, sensitive, and incredibly rich. School dances, babysitting, peer pressure, prejudice, academic honesty, and her mother's breast cancer all add to Katie's problems. But Katie is courageous and strong. She makes the right choices, and she is charming. The author, who grew up with dyslexia and is a learning disabilities teacher consultant, provides useful factual information about dyslexia. And she mentions such famous dyslexics as Cher, General George Patton, and Hans Christian Andersen. Through a girl's perspective, she teaches "that if you work hard, believe in yourself, and persevere, you can accomplish anything you set your mind to."

Subjects: dyslexia, learning disabled, middle school, popularity, self-perception, special education

85 Janover, Caroline. *Zipper: The Kid with ADHD*. Woodbine House. 1997. Paperback 164pp. Ages: 9–12. ISBN: 0–933149–95–6 $11.95. Illustrated by Rick Powell.

Fifth-grader Zachary "Zipper" Winson's thoughts bounce in his brain like a pinball machine. He has attention-deficit hyperactivity disorder. He forgets school assignments, frustrates his teacher and baseball coach, acts impulsively, alienates his classmates, has difficulty organizing activities and tasks, and annoys his family. But Zipper is intelligent, creative, and well intentioned. He's a strong pitcher and a talented drummer. One of his friends is Pete, a retired jazz musician who believes in him and teaches him about music and goals. Another friend is Josh, a dyslexic boy who helps him understand his disorder and take control of his life. This uplifting and realistic story presents ADHD as a condition that can be adjusted through behavioral changes, organizational techniques, and, sometimes, medication. It teaches understanding and acceptance of children with learning disabilities. Youngsters with ADHD will relate to Zipper's experiences and will be reassured by his progress. An appendix offers additional information about

ADHD, a list of resources and organizations, and suggested reading for parents, teachers, and young people.

Subjects: attention-deficit hyperactivity disorder, baseball, dyslexia, elementary school, learning disabled, music, sports

86 Johnson, Angela. *Humming Whispers*. Orchard Books. 1995. Hardcover 121pp. Ages: 9–12. ISBN: 0–531–08748–4 $14.95.

Twenty-four-year-old Nicole became schizophrenic when she was fourteen. Her younger sister, Sophy, who is fourteen now, fears that she, too, will hear the "whispers." She and Nicole have lived with their Aunt Shirley ever since their parents were killed in a car accident ten years ago. Aunt Shirley is very supportive, as are Nicole's boyfriend and their elderly neighbor, Miss Onyx. Sophy is a promising dancer, and Miss Onyx encourages Sophy to pursue her dream of becoming a dancer. Dancing gives Sophy the only peace and hope she knows. Sophy is unconditionally devoted to Nicole, but she feels powerless to help her. Sophy's unspoken fear that she will end up like her sister grows as she begins to see a changed face in the mirror. She starts shoplifting, hides the items under her bed, and lies to Nicole about them. Unforeseeably, it is Nicole who helps Sophy see that she must face her fear and focus on her future. The stream-of-consciousness style of Sophy's present-tense narrative is often disturbing, yet at times it is beautiful and hopeful. This brief novel explores the effects of schizophrenia on family members and close friends.

Subjects: African Americans, dance, emotional problems, mentally ill, schizophrenia, siblings

87 Jordan, Sherryl. *The Raging Quiet*. Simon & Schuster. 1999. Hardcover 272pp. Ages: 12 and up. ISBN: 0–689–82140–9 $17.00.

New Zealand author Sherryl Jordan has set this irresistible historical novel filled with romance and suspense in an ancient time and place. Sixteen-year-old Marnie reluctantly marries Isake, who is twice her age, to save her family from starvation. Isake is the lord of her parents' farm. He takes her to a remote fishing hamlet and two days later, while thatching the roof, falls to his death. The villagers are suspicious of Marnie's role in his death, and they shun her even more when she befriends Raven, a strange, mad boy who they believe to be possessed by the devil. Marnie discovers that Raven is not mad, but deaf, and his bursts of anger come from his inability to communicate and the "raging quiet within" him. She develops a system of hand signs. Through communication, Raven is transformed and their relationship grows into tenderhearted love. Seeing this, her hateful brother-in-law and the villagers accuse her of witchcraft and demand a trial where the test of the iron bar will determine her fate. Marnie is a remarkable, open-minded, courageous character who is determined that neither she nor Raven will become victims of ignorance and hatred. The author has experienced difficulties, disappointments, joy, and success working with deaf children in schools and consequently provides accurate details about the life of a deaf person. Her spirited, expressive prose style draws young adult readers into this compelling tale about Marnie and Raven, who are not afraid of being different.

Subjects: deaf, historical fiction, physically handicapped, sign language

88 Karim, Robert. *Mandy Sue Day*. Clarion Books. 1994. Hardcover 32pp. Ages: 5–8. ISBN: 0–395–66155–2. Out-of-print. Illustrated by Karen Ritz.

In Mandy Sue's large family, each child has a special day, free from farm chores and home schooling. Mandy Sue chooses to spend her day feeding, grooming, and riding her horse, Ben. She is competent, self-sufficient, and independent. She uses sensory detail to describe brushing Ben's knotted mane, bribing him with sugar cubes, clip-clopping through crunching leaves, and galloping with the wind across the plains. Back home, after chicken dinner and peach pie with a candle, Mandy Sue asks if she can sleep in the barn loft. Only when her little brother offers her a flashlight is it revealed that Mandy Sue is blind. The appealing prose poem brings Mandy Sue's world to life and conveys her happiness and her equestrian abilities. The detailed watercolors of Mandy Sue and the Indian Summer day on the farm landscape are resplendent.

Subjects: blind, horses, physically handicapped

89 Kehret, Peg. *My Brother Made Me Do It*. Minstrel. 2000. Hardcover 130pp. Ages: 9–12. ISBN: 0–671–03418–9 $16.00.

Fifth-grader Julie Welch and eighty-nine-year-old Mrs. Kaplan, who lives in the Shady Villa Care Center in Kansas, are pen pals because of Julie's school writing project. Julie's teacher requires her students to ask their pen pals specific questions. First, Julie introduces herself and tells about her sneaky, devious nine-year-old brother, Frankie, who always gets her into trouble. She also tells that he is memorizing all the topic headings in their set of encyclopedias. In answer to Julie's questions, she discovers that Mrs. Kaplan lived on the Isthmus of Panama when her father was involved in building the Panama Canal. Mrs. Kaplan also lived in a log cabin in Alaska; went on camera safaris to Africa; had a famous hymn writer, Fanny Crosby, for a friend; and even had a trained pet pig. Julie writes to Mrs. Kaplan about everything, including her secrets. Mrs. Kaplan is the first person she tells about her painful juvenile rheumatoid arthritis. Mrs. Kaplan understands. She has arthritis, too. Mrs. Kaplan encourages Julie and gives her ideas about running for student council. Through the personal letters, readers learn Julie's thoughts and feelings. She is worried about being able to compete in the fun run at school because her legs hurt so much, but Frankie, her brother, boosts her self-confidence. She decides to try it on crutches. With Frankie's support and that of her friends, she completes the four-mile race. The last letters are from Mrs. Kaplan's daughter, written after Mrs. Kaplan's death. She returns all of Julie's letters to her along with a copy of the obituary, which said Mrs. Kaplan was a homemaker who lived her whole life in Kansas. At first Julie is disappointed, thinking Mrs. Kaplan had lied to her. But she realizes that Mrs. Kaplan had a fertile imagination and was reliving a happy time of her life when she told her daughter wonderful stories. Julie's teacher points out that the class learned a lot from Mrs. Kaplan's letters. They had fun reading about the Panama Canal, Africa, Alaska, Fanny Crosby, and even pigs. Mrs. Kaplan didn't lie to Julie. She just made up stories to enrich Julie's life. The references to juvenile rheumatoid arthritis are accurate, and Julie's pain, fear, and treatments are authentic. An author's note on juvenile arthritis and where to find out more information conclude this heartwarming, inspirational yet humorous book.

Subjects: elementary school, intergenerational relationships, juvenile rheumatoid arthritis, physically handicapped, siblings

90 King-Smith, Dick. *Spider Sparrow*. Crow Publishers. 1998. Hardcover 163pp. Ages: 12 and up. ISBN: 0–517–80043–8 $16.95.

In the World War II English countryside, Spider, an abandoned baby boy, is adopted by Tom and Kathie Sparrow, a childless shepherd and his wife. Spider is not normal. At age two he doesn't speak but can imitate exactly the hoot of an owl, the call of a cuckoo, and the meow of a cat. His scuttling on his hands and feet earns him the nickname "Spider," and by the age of six he walks in a curious, bent-forward, flat-footed, and turned-out manner. The village boys copy his walk and snigger at him. Most of the adults are kind, but some find Spider repellant. Spider is "half-witted" and can't learn like other children. He will never be fit to go to school. Spider's parents cherish him and find jobs that he can do around the farm. He is an excellent crowstarver (one who scares off crows from newly planted fields). Spider has a special gift. He can mimic animal sounds and has the amazing ability to communicate with any animal. Animals are drawn to him. He hand feeds a fox, comforts a lambing ewe, and "gentles" wild broncos. He also creates woodcarvings of the animals. Because Spider is mentally subnormal, yet displays outstanding talent in a particular area, Mrs. Yorke, the wife of the gentleman farmer who is Sparrow's employer, calls Spider an idiot savant. Spider is happy, slow, and dependable. When he is sixteen, a heart defect causes his death. In his sixteen years, mentally slow Spider faced every day with contentment and courage and left an unforgettable impact on all who knew him.

Subjects: adoption, England, gifted and talented, historical fiction, mentally handicapped, nature

91   Klass, Sheila Solomon. *Little Women Next Door*. Holiday House. 2000. Hardcover 188pp. Ages: 8–12. ISBN: 0-8234-1472-8 $15.95.

It's 1843 near Harvard, Massachusetts, about fifteen miles from Concord, and lonely, eleven-year-old Susan Wilson is thrilled when new neighbors move nextdoor. Susan stammers, is shy, and hasn't had many opportunities to meet people or to make friends. The new neighbors are future-author Louisa May Alcott and her family, who have moved to the area to establish an experimental utopian community, to be called the Fruitlands. Susan befriends Louisa; attends the school taught by Louisa's father, Bronson Alcott, and Charles Lane; is treated to regular visits from Henry David Thoreau and Ralph Waldo Emerson; and learns about Transcendentalist philosophies. On one of his visits Thoreau points out to Susan that she is "one of a long line of illustrious stammerers" that includes the great Greek orator Demosthenes. Susan is surprised at the radical Transcendentalist ideas about dress, diet, and family and farm life. The Transcendentalists do not drink milk or wear wool. They do not use any animal products or by-products at all. They even try to farm without plow animals. And so their farm fails in the first year. Nevertheless Susan's adventures playing and exploring with the Alcotts allow her to blossom, and she defeats her stammer. This engaging historical novel will especially appeal to fans of Louisa May Alcott and *Little Women*. An author's note explains more about Transcendentalism and what happened to the Fruitlands family. Other valuable sources of information are also suggested.

Subjects: historical fiction, Massachusetts, physically handicapped, speech disorders

92   Kline, Suzy. *Mary Marony and the Snake*. G. P. Putnam's Sons. 1992. Hardcover 64pp. Ages: 8–12. ISBN: 0–399–22044–5. Out of print. Illustrated by Blanche Sims.

Mary Marony is worried about starting second grade in a new school, where her teacher and classmates won't know about her problem and understand. Mary stutters. Some of the children are friendly and sympathetic, but Marvin Higgins is mean and makes fun of her. Mary's loving mother and the school's speech therapist, whom she likes, offer her encouragement and help. When Marvin's dad brings a garter snake to school and it escapes from the terrarium, everyone is terrified, especially Marvin. It is brave Mary who saves the day. Mary's mother has a garden and has taught Mary how to handle garter snakes. Mary captures the runaway snake, earns the respect of her new classmates, and realizes that things will be okay in second grade. Amusing pencil drawings and the easy text make clear Mary's anxiety, anger, and accomplishment. The six short chapters are just right for children who are beginning to read independently.

Subjects: elementary school, physically handicapped, speech disorders, stuttering, teachers

93   Konigsburg, E. L. *Silent to the Bone*. Atheneum. 2000. Hardcover 261pp. Ages: 9–12. ISBN: 0–689–83601–5 $16.00.

Two-time Newbery medal winner Konigsburg's story is dark and gripping. It begins with a tape of the 911 call from thirteen-year-old Branwell Zamborska because his baby sister, Nikki, has stopped breathing. When Branwell is unable to speak, Vivian, the English au pair, comes on the line to tell the emergency operator that Branwell dropped the baby and shook her. Nikki is taken to the hospital and Branwell to a juvenile behavior center. The story is told by Branwell's sharply observant best friend, Conner, who visits the behavior center and works out a system whereby he gets Branwell to communicate by blinking his eyes at words and letters on flash cards. With the help of Conner's half-sister, Margaret, he investigates the events leading up to Branwell's silence and finds out what really happened on the Wednesday afternoon of the 911 call. It is shame that caused Branwell's mutism. At first he didn't speak about Vivian's afternoons with the pizza deliveryman, his own relationship with her, and her mistreating the baby. But after the baby is injured, he cannot speak. Conner helps Branwell recover and speak the truth about Vivian. Nikki also recovers, and in the touching final scene Branwell's genuine love of Nikki is evident.

Branwell's mutism is an articulate part of this complex story about adolescent emotions and confusions.

Subjects: elective mutism, emotional problems, healthcare facilities, siblings

94 Konigsburg, E. L. *The View from Saturday.* Atheneum. 1996. Hardcover 163pp. Ages: 8–12. ISBN: 0–689–80993–X $16.00.

Epiphany Middle School's sixth-grade Academic Bowl team is made up of four very bright students and coached by Mrs. Olinski, a paraplegic. Though at first the students seem to be quite different, they become soul mates. Ethan is the kind of boy who still asks the question "Now what?" instead of "So what?" Nadia is a beautiful girl who helped her father save hatchling sea turtles on the Florida coast. Noah is a resourceful team member who, by accident, was the best man at the wedding of Ethan's grandmother and Nadia's grandfather. And Julian is an East Indian boy, newly arrived to America, who is so weird that he wears shorts and knee socks and carries a leather book bag. Mrs. Olinski has returned to teaching after an automobile accident that left her paralyzed from the waist down. She is the first teacher Epiphany ever had who taught from a wheelchair. She introduces herself to the class as "one of those people who gets to use all those good parking spaces at the mall." She is not wounded by the word *cripple,* but by the manner of its delivery. The dynamic team wins the sixth-grade competition and, to everyone's surprise, beats the seventh and eighth grades, too. The four children and their teacher complete important journeys along the way. They learn about teamwork, confidence, and success. They find kindness in others and how to look for it in themselves.

Subjects: gifted and talented, middle school, physically handicapped, teachers, wheelchairs

95 Kornblatt, Marc. *Understanding Buddy.* McElderry Books. 2001. Hardcover 113pp. Ages: 8–12. ISBN: 0–689–83215–X $16.00.

The new boy in fifth grade, Buddy White, is strange. He is so withdrawn that he doesn't talk or even smile. When approached, he turns away or punches. Only Sam Keeperman knows what's troubling Buddy. Last summer Buddy's mother, who was the Keeperman's cleaning lady, was killed in a car accident. Sam reaches out to Buddy and sticks up for him when other kids tease him. In so doing, Sam's relationship with his best friend, Alex, is threatened, a fistfight erupts, and the boys are kicked off the soccer team.

Sam's first-person narrative touches on religious and class differences. Sam is Jewish. Buddy is a Jehovah's Witness and poor. He shows up at school wearing Sam's old clothes. Sam, who is always thinking, uses his Hebrew class to raise some religious questions, such as Where do the souls of dead people go? and What is heaven? Sam manages to get close to Buddy as Buddy struggles with his loss, comes out of his shell, and starts to speak again. Sam learns what it means to lose someone you love and that some things "make no sense, and no matter how hard you try to understand them they may never make sense, but they can still make you laugh. Or cry."

Subjects: death, elective mutism, elementary school, grief, religions

96   Kroll, Virginia. *Naomi Knows It's Springtime*. Boyds Mills Press. 1993. Hardcover 32pp. Ages: 5–8. ISBN: 1–56397–006–6. Out of print. Illustrated by Jill Kastner.

Spring is described in rhythmic, repetitive language the way Naomi experiences it. She feels the air kiss her cheeks. She hears the squeaks of newborn nestlings. She sails and spins in the tire swing. She smells lilies and lilacs and feels the tickle of a ladybug on her hand. Only when a neighbor sighs, "If only Naomi could see the blue in the sky!" do readers learn that Naomi is blind. Naomi smiles and responds, "If only Mrs. Jensen could see the rainbow in my mind!" Misty, impressionistic oil paintings grace this positive, powerful picture of a blind girl's spring.

Subjects: blind, nature, physically handicapped

97   Kurtz, Jane. *The Storyteller's Beads*. Harcourt Brace & Co. 1998. Hardcover 128pp. Ages: 8–12. ISBN: 0–15–201074–2 $15.00.

This is the story of the dangerous journey of two refugee girls during the political strife and famine in Ethiopia in the 1980s. Sahay and her uncle, who are from the northern Ethiopian Christian Kemant community, are the only survivors of their massacred family. Rahel, who is blind, and her brother are Jewish and named *Falasha*, or strangers, by Sahay's people. The two ethnic groups have been taught to mistrust each other and call each other *buda*, or possessed of the evil eye. Rahel has only her flute and her grandmother's string of beads, which symbolize her family and faith. Sahay's uncle and Rahel's brother are forced to turn back at the border and the two girls are thrown together. The barrier between the girls breaks down when Sahay becomes Rahel's guide until they reach the refugee camp at Umm Rekuba. They survive terror, despair, and anger and eventually escape to Jerusalem in a clandestine Israeli airlift. This hopeful novel effectively conveys the strength and richness of the Ethiopian cultures and the prejudices that keep them apart. Ethiopian language is integrated into the text, and a glossary, map, and background notes help readers accompany the girls on their journey and understand a time and place of which most U.S. children know little.

Subjects: Africa, blind, Ethiopia, Israel, music, physically handicapped, religions, storytellers

98 Lakin, Pat. *Dad and Me in the Morning*. Albert Whitman, 1994. Hardcover 32pp. Ages: 4–8. ISBN: 0–8075–1419–5 $14.95. Illustrated by Robert C. Steele.

Jacob rises early before dawn, gets dressed, puts on his hearing aids, and wakes up his dad for a special walk to the beach to watch the sunrise. They communicate by signing, speaking, lip-reading, gesturing, and making secret signals. A baby bunny hiding in the flowers, the smell of pine trees, wading barefoot in the cold water, scooting hermit crabs, clouds that look like popcorn, and the warm sun are gloriously painted in Jacob's soundless world. The straightforward text is placed on watercolored rectangles opposite the full-page peaceful nature scenes. This is a positive story based on the relationship between a deaf boy and his father.

Subjects: deaf, nature, physically handicapped, sign language

99 Lang, Glenna. *Looking Out for Sarah*. Charlesbridge. 2001. Hardcover 32pp. Ages: 5–8. ISBN: 0–88106–647–8 $15.95. Illustrated by the author.

Shopping at the grocery store, visiting the post office, and riding the train are seen through Perry's eyes. Perry is Sarah Gregory Smith's guide dog. Perry is a friendly seven-year-old black Labrador retriever. He likes taking walks, chasing balls, and eating bagels. He attended a guide dog school run by Guiding Eyes for the Blind in Yorktown Heights, New York, and graduated after six months of hard training. Sarah lost her sight as an adult from diabetes. She teaches music and dance and performs folk concerts in schools for children. After the concerts, the children ask her many questions. And Perry falls asleep. She describes and Perry dreams about the great adventure they had walking 300 miles from Boston to New York to show the world what a guide dog can do for a blind person. They even met the mayor of New York City. Important information about guide dogs is smoothly integrated throughout, such as the facts that they are allowed in stores and restaurants and that they should not be petted or handled while they are working. In writing this book, the author interviewed and observed many guide dogs and their owners and researched the subject at the Perkins School for the Blind. The full-page, bold gouache paintings help show the unique bond between a woman who manages without eyesight and the dog that helps her do it.

Subjects: blind, dance, dogs—service, music, New York City, physically handicapped, service dogs

100 Lawrence, Iain. *Ghost Boy*. Delacorte Press. 2000. Hardcover 336pp. Ages: 12 and up. ISBN: 0–385–32739–0 $15.95.

Harold Kline is fourteen years old, an albino, and a runaway from his small midwestern town where people taunt him and call him "Ghost Boy" or "Maggot" because he is "white as chalk." Life there is also unbearable because his father and brother were lost in World War II and his mother re-married a man who doesn't understand him. When Hunter and Greens Traveling Circus comes to town, Harold joins the troupe of colorful per-formers, hoping to find acceptance. The characters are fascinating and well defined. The midget Princess Minikin and her man-beast companion, Fossil Man, treat him almost like a son. He falls in love with beautiful Flip, the horse trainer, and is enchanted by the Indian legends of Thunder Wakes Him. He is amazed by Gypsy Magda and marvels at the Cannibal King, who is also an albino. Harold earns their respect by teaching the elephants to play baseball. But he discovers that even in the circus there are two groups, the freaks and everyone else. He learns that beauty and freakishness are deter-mined by a person's inner nature and not by outward appearance. This strange novel appeals because of its circus scenes and its theme of an out-cast teenager's search for love and happiness. The author's acknowledg-ments explain the inspiration for the story, which was an English circus where elephants played cricket. Also included is information about albi-nism and NOAH, the National Organization of Albinism and Hypopigmentation.

Subjects: albinism, self-perception, skin

101 Lears, Laurie. *Ben Has Something to Say*. Albert Whitman & Co. 2000. Hardcover 32pp. Ages: 5–8. ISBN: 0–8075–0633–8 $14.95. Il-lustrated by Karen Ritz.

Ben is a good reader, but he does not like to read aloud or even talk to other children at school because he stutters. Every Friday, Ben and his dad visit Wayne's junkyard to get car parts. Ben tells his dad all about his day. Ben's dad never laughs or teases when Ben's words get stuck. Ben befriends the junkyard dog, Spike. He brings a rubber bone and a blanket, refills Spike's water dish, and really becomes attached to the dog. Ben tries to talk to Mr. Wayne about taking better care of the dog, but he's too ashamed to speak. When the junkyard is robbed and Spike doesn't even bark, Mr. Wayne threatens to take Spike to the pound. Now Ben knows he has to speak. What he has to say is more important than the way he says it. He finds the courage to ask if he can buy Spike. His dad agrees, and on the ride home Ben decides he might be brave enough to tell his friends at school about his new dog. The realistic watercolor illustrations represent Ben's embarrassment at school, his patient father, his concern for Spike, and his newly found confidence. A foreword for adults or older readers gives information about stuttering and advice for those who know someone who stutters. Additional resources, including organizations and Web sites, are listed at the end of the book.

Subjects: dogs, physically handicapped, speech disorders

102 Lears, Laurie. *Ian's Walk: A Story about Autism*. Albert Whitman. 1998. Hardcover 32pp. Ages: 4–8. ISBN: 0-8075-3480-3 $14.95. Illustrated by Karen Ritz.

This book is more than the story of Ian's walk. It is a description of how Ian's autism affects his sister, Julie. It is also a clear explanation of autistic disorder for readers of all ages. Julie and her older sister, Tara, reluctantly agree to let Ian walk with them to the park. Julie describes how Ian sees, hears, smells, feels, and tastes things differently from most people. For example, at Mrs. Potter's flower stand Ian wrinkles his nose and turns away from a bouquet of lilacs. Instead, as they walk past the post office, he puts his nose against the warm bricks and sniffs the wall. Julie becomes frustrated and impatient. She is embarrassed and hopes that no one will notice. But when Ian wanders away, it is her close observations of him that help her find him. She knows what Ian likes to do and discovers him lying under the old bell in the center of the park making the big gong move back and forth. They walk home the way Ian likes. They bypass the flower stand and stop at the post office, where Ian sniffs the bricks and this time Julie doesn't care who's watching. Ian's smile at the end of the book says that it was a good walk. The story is straightforward and honest. It evokes compassion without pity. The illustrations are spontaneous and genuine, and Ian's postures are accurate and authentic. Ian is a real child who just interacts with life from a different perspective. Preliminary notes written by professional pediatric caregivers sensitize readers to the resentment, anger, and isolation that siblings of children with autism often feel, as well as their strong feelings of loyalty, responsibility, and love.

Subjects: autism, siblings

103 Lears, Laurie. *Waiting for Mr. Goose*. Albert Whitman. 1999. Hardcover 32pp. Ages: 5–8. ISBN: 0–8075–8628–5 $14.95. Illustrated by Karen Ritz.

In school or at home, someone is always telling Stephen to slow down, sit still, or pay attention. Stephen often feels that he can't do anything right. He enjoys playing along the banks of the pond near his home where he can be free. One day he discovers a goose that is limping because of a metal chain clamped on its leg. Stephen's mom calls a man from the nature center who comes to help, but he gives up when he can't catch the goose. But Stephen won't give up. He tries to catch the injured goose by tricking it and chasing it. When that doesn't work, he realizes that he'll have to gain the goose's trust by putting out corn every day and waiting. But Stephen knows he's not good at waiting. He focuses on his problem and develops enough patience to eventually rescue the goose. The realistic watercolor illustrations present Stephen as a caring and warm character. An introductory note discusses attention-deficit hyperactivity disorder (ADHD), although it is never mentioned in the text.

Subjects: birds, attention-deficit hyperactivity disorder, learning disabled

104 Lee, Jeanne M. *Silent Lotus*. Farrar, Straus & Giroux. 1991. Paperback 32pp. Ages: 5–8. ISBN: 0–374–46646–7 $5.95. Illustrated by the author.

Lotus is a young Cambodian girl who cannot hear or speak. She loves to mimic the graceful movements of the herons, cranes, and egrets that live in the lakes near her home. She understands her parents' gestures and learns to represent her name with her hands. But Lotus is lonely and unhappy because the other children ignore her and run away. Seeing her unhappiness, her parents take her to the temple hoping for a miracle. There she sees the temple dancers, feels the vibrations of the drums and cymbals, and imitates the dancers' movements. She captures the attention of the king, and he arranges for her to learn to dance the legends of the gods and kings. In time, she performs for the royal court and becomes the most famous dancer in the Khmer kingdom. The artwork, which features flat, brilliantly colored, stylized paintings of the ancient Cambodian countryside and court life, was inspired by the decoration on the twelfth-century temple at Angkor Wat. This simple fairy tale quietly tells of the transformation of a lonely girl without language into a successful woman despite her disability.

Subjects: birds, Cambodia, dance, deaf, legends, music, mutism, physically handicapped

105   Lester, Helen. *Hooway for Wodney Wat*. Houghton Mifflin. 1999. Hardcover 32pp. Ages: 4–8. ISBN: 0–395–92392–1 $15.00. Illustrated by Lynn Munsinger.

Timid Rodney Rat can't pronounce the letter "r," and the other rodents in his class tease him relentlessly. He's so distraught that he has to gnaw his lunch alone and hide inside his jacket at recess. When a new rodent, Camilla Capybara, barges into the classroom and announces that she is bigger, meaner, and smarter than anyone else, every rodent is afraid. Wodney unwittingly gets the better of the mean Camilla when he leads a humorous game of Simon Says. Wodney's surprising wordplay saves the whole class from Camilla's bullying ways. The well-detailed, comical watercolors give each rodent personality in this perfect read-aloud book.

Subjects: bullies, elementary school, physically handicapped, speech disorders

106   Lowry, Lois. *Gathering Blue*. Houghton Mifflin. 2000. Hardcover 224pp. Ages: 9 and up. ISBN: 0–618–05581–9 $15.00.

This provocative story is set in a possible future world that has suffered a disaster and has regressed to a primitive, technology-free state. It is a world ruled by cruelty and deceit, one where the weak and physically flawed are shunned or discarded. Young Kira, born with a deformed leg and now suddenly orphaned, fears she will be cast out of the community. However, her amazing talent for embroidery and weaving is recognized by the society's Council of Guardians. She is taken to live at the magnificent Council Edifice, where her job is to repair and restore the precious ceremonial robe that the Singer wears during the annual Ruin Song Gathering. The robe depicts the history of her community's multiple rises and falls. It's up to Kira to complete the blank panels of the garment, which will depict the future. Also living in the Edifice are Thomas, an orphan, whose job it is to carve the Singer's staff, and tiny Jo, another orphan, who sings like an angel and is being trained to be the next Singer. The power-hungry Guardians seem to be kind but are really capturing the creative gifts of the three young artists for their own needs. Kira pieces together the truth about her society after her cheerful young friend, Matt, returns from yonder with the plant used to make the blue dye she needs for coloring the future on the robe. Matt describes yonder as a place where the people are nice and quiet, but broken like Kira. Matt also brings a sightless old man who turns out to be Kira's father, whom she believed was killed by beasts. Kira thinks of leaving with her father but has the vision to remain to weave colors into the scenes of beauty that will transform her society. Lowry's powerful story will stimulate plenty of thought and discussion about Kira's world and her future.

Subjects: blind, fantasy, physically handicapped

107 Maguire, Gregory. *Missing Sisters*. Hyperion. 1998. Paperback 152pp. Ages: 10 and up. ISBN: 0–7868–1273–7 $4.95.

In upstate New York in 1968, twelve-year-old Alice Colossus is living in an orphanage run by nuns. She has never been adopted because she has speech and hearing impairments and quite a feisty personality. She makes a pact with God that she won't consider adoption until she knows that her closest friend, Sister Vincent de Paul, who was injured in a fire, will recover. Alice attends a summer camp and is mistaken for another girl, Miami Shaw, who turns out to be the identical twin sister Alice didn't know she had. Miami has no disabilities and has a loving adoptive family, but with four adopted children and their first biological child on the way, they can't take Alice in. The girls make a lot of plans to be together. They even put a letter in the newspaper explaining that they are twins who do not want to be separated. And finally Alice discovers that Sister Vincent de Paul is recovering in a nursing home. Much relieved, Alice is adopted by a family who becomes interested in her because of the letter in the paper. Alice's disability is the source of some humorous scenes. The nuns always correct her, but her "zigzaggy" speech doesn't bother her that much. She has a beautiful singing voice and is quite a hit as Eliza Dolittle, the flower girl, in *My Fair Lady*.

Subjects: adoption, deaf, music, physically handicapped, siblings, theatre, twins

108 Mahony, Mary. *There's an "S" on My Back: "S" is for Scoliosis.* Redding Press. 1999. Paperback 201pp. Ages: 9–12. ISBN: 0–9658879–1–X $14.95.

In this heart-warming book, recommended by the National Scoliosis Foundation, eleven-year-old Maisey MacGuire is diagnosed with idiopathic scoliosis and has to wear a brace on her back. At first it makes her angry and very uneasy. It is embarrassing because none of the other kids in her fifth-grade class had to wear anything like it, and it is "challenging her wardrobe." Maisey is also dyslexic, though she is a good student and her reading has improved. She feels better about wearing the brace when she discovers that some of her classmates had worn braces for different problems. Her friends care about her and seem to understand how she feels. And it helps that Maisey can do most of the things she did before she got the brace, like playing baseball and going to environmental camp. Regular visits to Dr. Bones indicate that the brace is only partially successful at keeping her spine from any further curving. Her brace needs to be modified often. Meanwhile she moves on to middle school, where she studies the Middle East, reads *To Kill a Mockingbird*, and builds scenery for *You're a Good Man, Charlie Brown*. Dr. Bones decreases her time out of the brace when X rays reveal increasing rotation of her spine. Finally, at the end of seventh grade, surgery is the only alternative for Maisey. Her hospital experience is described very accurately. An epilogue tells that Maisy recovered nicely from the spinal fusion and a year later was back to all her normal activities. The author draws on her experience as the mother of a girl with scoliosis and offers keen insight into the onset, progression, and treatment of this congenital spine deformity. She also gives advice on the importance of bracing in the life of a scoliosis patient.

Subjects: dyslexia, elementary school, healthcare facilities, learning disabled, middle school, scoliosis

109 Marsden, John. *Checkers*. Random House. 1996. Paperback 122pp. Ages: 12 and up. ISBN: 0–440–22869–3 $4.99.

In this suspense story set in Australia, a nameless fifteen-year-old girl describes her peers in group therapy in a mental hospital and recounts the events leading to her institutionalization. She was smart, happy, and privileged until her businessman father became involved in a national financial scandal. Her joy was Checkers, a playful puppy that her father brought home on the day he announced that he had closed a very lucrative, high-profile business contract. The contract was illegally acquired through dishonest transactions with the Australian premier, who denied ever having met her business executive father. After months of investigation the girl accidentally reveals that Checkers was a gift from the premier. This confirms her father's guilt, and in uncontrolled anger he kills her dog. Apparently she has a mental breakdown after this and is sent to a psychiatric hospital. The other patients in her therapy group include obsessive-compulsive Daniel, anorexic Oliver, school-phobic Emine, and Esther, who thinks a furry animal lives in her head. Although they all discuss their problems freely in group sessions, it takes a long time for the girl to speak. It is through her diary entries that her pain and sadness owing to adult corruption and the collapse of her family are revealed.

Subjects: Australia, dogs, eating disorders, emotional problems, healthcare facilities, mentally ill, mystery, obsessive-compulsive disorder

110   Martin, Ann M. *Abby's Twin* (Baby-Sitters Club series #104). Scholastic. 1997. Paperback 127pp. Ages: 9–12. ISBN: 0–590–69210–0 $3.99.

Eighth graders Anna and Abby Stevenson are twins. Both are members of the Baby-Sitters Club. Abby is an athlete, and Anna is a musician who lives to play her violin. In a routine school health check, a curve is discovered in Anna's back. It is recommended that she see Dr. Sherman, an orthopedist, who diagnoses scoliosis and prescribes a brace. She explains Anna's condition and thoroughly describes the bracing treatment. Abby seems to be more devastated than Anna about it all and goes overboard in trying to cheer Anna and support her. Anna just wants to be alone for a time, and even though they have that special twin bond, she accuses Abby of not really knowing her. The girls don't speak to each other for a week. They are both angry, hurt, and confused. Mary Anne, a fellow babysitter, suggests to Abby that Anna probably doesn't understand how Abby wants to help and that she must feel helpless seeing her twin go through something she can't do anything about. Abby needn't feel guilty that this happened to Anna or fear that they won't be twins anymore. Anna confides to Abby that all the overprotecting makes her feel as though her normal life has ended. Anna reassures Abby that they can make it through the rough times ahead and that this is what being twins is all about. An author's note explains that her readers suggested that she write a book about scoliosis and that she hopes her book will help them understand scoliosis better. Notebook pages pose questions about Anna's condition for readers to consider.

Subjects: middle school, physically handicapped, scoliosis, siblings, twins

111   Martin, Ann M. *Dawn and Whitney: Friends Forever* (Baby-Sitters Club series #77). Scholastic. 1994. Paperback 144pp. Ages: 8–12. ISBN: 0–590–48221–1 $3.99.

In #77 of the Baby-Sitters Club series, Dawn is hired as a sitter/companion for twelve-year-old Whitney, in the afternoons for a few weeks during the summer. Whitney has Down syndrome and has been attending a special school but is being switched into the public school system. Here she will be mainstreamed, except for some special classes, like speech therapy. Whitney's parents tell her that Dawn is her new friend, rather than a babysitter. Whitney feels she doesn't need a babysitter now that she's graduating to public school. Dawn is a little worried because she has never met anyone with Down syndrome and doesn't know what to expect. Whitney's father describes his daughter's disability and her personality to Dawn before the girls meet. Dawn likes Whitney. They have great times together, and Dawn discovers that Whitney isn't that different. She, like all of Dawn's friends, is grown-up in many ways and so young in others. The difference is that "for Whitney, the grown-up part of her mind could only grow up so much." Whitney gives Dawn a Best Friends necklace, and Dawn realizes that Whitney had started out as a job but now is a friend. When Whitney insists on having another ice cream sandwich over Dawn's objections, Dawn blurts out that she is Whitney's babysitter and that is why she can't have more ice cream. Dawn is horrified at what she said, and Whitney is humiliated and angry. After several days of Whitney not speaking to Dawn and Whitney finally proving that she is grown-up enough to baby-sit, Whitney and Dawn become friends again. Whitney even becomes an honorary member of the Baby-Sitters Club. Realistic dialogue and characters help create this refreshing story about a girl with Down syndrome.

Subjects: Down syndrome, mentally handicapped, special education

112   Martin, Ann M. *Kristy and the Secret of Susan* (Baby-Sitters Club series #32). Scholastic. 1990. Paperback 145pp. Ages: 8–12. ISBN: 0–590–42496–3 $3.50.

Eighth grader Kristy's newest babysitting charge is eight-year-old Susan Felder. Susan can't communicate with anyone, although she can play the piano and sing beautifully. Susan is autistic. She lives in her own world and doesn't want to leave it. Susan's mother carefully describes Susan's disability to Kristy. Susan exhibits strange behaviors, she rarely makes eye contact with anyone, she doesn't like to be hugged or touched, and her future looks bleak. She does, however, have special talents. She astonishes everyone, including her teachers and doctors, because she can play any new piece of music after hearing it only once. She also has a calendar in her head. She can tell the day of the week that any date fell on. She seems to have memorized a perpetual calendar. Susan's parents are sending Susan to a special school with a strong music program, hoping that through music Susan will acquire some meaningful language as well as some social skills. Music may be the way to reach her. Kristy is fascinated by Susan and decides to try to convince the Felders that Susan can live and learn and make friends at home. She wouldn't have to attend the special school. She could make friends at Stonybrook Elementary School. She wouldn't have to be an outcast. Kristy wants to show everyone just how "normal" Susan could be. In the process, Kristy learns a lot. She becomes angry when kids at Stonybrook make fun of the special class, and she becomes even more upset when kids make a sideshow of Susan by paying a dollar to see her play the piano or recite dates. Kristy comes to realize that the students in the special class at Stonybrook are more advanced than Susan is. They talk, can learn, and are not locked up inside themselves. Kristy further discovers that just by introducing Susan to what a "normal" life is, Susan can't change. She "needs extra-extra-extra-extra special help." The new school is the best place for her. A relevant subplot involves the Hobarts, a family that recently moved to the neighborhood from Australia. At first they are all outcasts. Kids don't accept them because they are all different. But it turns out that they are not so different after all. They eventually fit in.

Subjects: Australia, autism, elementary school, middle school, music

113 Mayer, Gina, and Mercer Mayer. *A Very Special Critter*. Western Publishing Co. 1993. Paperback 24pp. Ages: 4–8. ISBN: 0–307–12763–X $3.29.

Little Critter is scared because Alex, the new student at school, is a very special critter who uses a wheelchair. Dad says just because he's in a wheelchair doesn't make him any different from the rest of the class. He may need some special help sometimes. The students are curious, but Alex doesn't mind their questions. He does need help sometimes, but so does Little Critter. At Halloween, Alex, dressed like a car, has the best costume in the whole school. The new critter is really one of the gang. This is an honest look at how children deal with the unknown, complete with typical Mercer Mayer humor.

Subjects: elementary school, physically handicapped, wheelchairs

114 Mazer, Harry. *The Wild Kid.* Simon & Schuster. 1998. Hardcover 103pp. Ages: 9 and up. ISBN: 0–689–80751–1 $15.00.

Sammy, a twelve-year-old boy with Down syndrome, gets lost in the woods and stumbles upon the hideout of Kevin, the "wild kid" or "k-man." Kevin is a reform school runaway. He holds Sammy hostage at first and treats him badly. He calls Sammy dumb. Sammy replies that he's young for his age and a special person. Kevin is afraid Sammy will blow his cover. But, slowly, they share stories and begin to depend on each other for survival. Kevin teaches Sammy about rabbits and berries in the woods, and Sammy, a Special Olympics swimmer, saves Kevin from drowning. Sammy wants to go home and devises a plan whereby Kevin should come live with him and be his brother. In the end, Kevin makes an anonymous phone call to the police. Sammy is rescued, and Kevin disappears back into the woods. When Sammy tells what happened, people don't really believe him. The psychologist says children of Sammy's mental abilities often use a survival mechanism whereby they imagine a safe world when they are in difficult situations. But Sammy's mom says, "he's more resourceful and smarter than people think." The thirteen-day adventure is told from Sammy's innocent point of view. The narrative is both suspenseful and poignant. Short chapters move the plot along in this story about trust and friendship between two misfit boys.

Subjects: Down syndrome, mentally handicapped

115 McElfresh, Lynn E. *Can You Feel the Thunder?* Simon & Schuster. 1999. Hardcover 144pp. Ages: 12 and up. ISBN: 0–689–82324–X $16.00.

Seventh grader Mic Parsons has an older sister, Stephanie, who is deaf and blind. They used to be close, but now she has become an embarrassment. He can't bear to have his friends see her because she makes funny sounds and bumps into things. And he is jealous over the extra attention she gets at home. She is the weirdest resident of his street, Bixby Court, until Vern Chortle moves into the neighborhood. Vern is a special education student with 382 pairs of strange socks, opera-loving parents, and a passion for baseball. He carries laminated maps and wears a beeping watch because of his dyscalculia, a math learning disability. At first Mic is turned off by Vern's friendliness and follows the rest of his buddies in making fun of Vern. He even calls him Nerd Boy. But Mic finds himself increasingly drawn to this uncommon boy and his family. They share many interests. Both boys have problems with math, and they both want to play baseball in the Pony League. Mic does eventually straighten out his priorities. His old friendships become less important as he accepts Vern's uniqueness and true friendship. And when Stephanie turns out to be the only one who can help him understand fractions, he comes to terms with his feelings about her disabilities and appreciates her special understanding of him and her resilient spirit. The fast-paced novel authentically describes the middle-school social scene and is straightforward about understanding people with disabilities and how they express themselves.

Subjects: baseball, blind, deaf, dyscalculia, learning disabled, middle school, physically handicapped, siblings, sports

116 McKay, Sharon. *Charlie Wilcox*. Stoddart Kids. 2000. Paperback 221pp. Ages: 10 and up. ISBN: 0–7737–6093–8. $7.95.

Fourteen-year-old Charlie Wilcox was born with a clubfoot. He yearns to go to the sea, on the ice, as a seal hunter off the coast of his native Newfoundland. His father and uncles are all sea captains, and Charlie wants to do the same. His "hip-hop disability" doesn't stop him from doing much. It is "no bother, none a t'all," even though some of his friends tease him and insult him about it. And he overhears his father say, "he's not made for the ice" because of his foot. His parents want him to have a better life. They arrange for him to have surgery to correct his clubfoot and then go to college. Determined to prove himself, Charlie stows away on what he thinks is a sealing ship, but it is actually a ship carrying soldiers to Europe to fight in World War I. Charlie struggles to survive as he waits to be shipped back home. He searches out the Newfoundland Regiment in France and works as an orderly in a mobile hospital unit. He heads for the front at the Battle of the Somme, where the men of the Newfoundland Regiment distinguished themselves as among the bravest soldiers in the war. Charlie witnesses the horrors of trench warfare, which are painted vividly in this adventure novel. He saves several friends' lives and proves his worth. With his great-great grandfather's spy glass, which was a gift from his father and which he vows he will never lose, he learns to "see through the glass, . . . not look . . . ," to see with his heart, his soul, and his eyes. After the war Charlie returns to his family in Newfoundland as a man. An author's note explains which parts of the story are fact and which ones are fiction. Charlie Wilcox did exist and he did have a clubfoot, but he never went to war. He did sail around the world. A postscript gives facts about the Battle of the Somme, and a glossary defines words that belong to Newfoundland's special language.

Subjects: historical fiction, Newfoundland, physically handicapped

117   McKenzie, Ellen Kindt. *Stargone John*. Henry Holt & Co. 1990. Hardcover 67pp. Ages: 4–8. ISBN: 0–606–02256–2 $13.95. Illustrated by William Low.

Six-year-old John is "just plain star gone." He may be learning disabled, yet he is gifted. Readers are never sure. The story takes place in the American Midwest at the turn of the century, when special needs children were not labeled, as they are today. John won't talk to anyone except his nine-year-old sister, Liza, and he is resistant to traditional teaching methods. He is ridiculed by his classmates and punished by his teacher in the one-room schoolhouse. Liza remembers Miss Mants, her teacher from last year, who became blind and then retired. She knows Miss Mants could teach John to read and cipher. They secretly go to visit her. John continues to go to her house, where through a kind of Braille, putting pinholes in paper, she shares the world of reading and writing with him. Dark, textured pencil drawings illustrate this gentle story of John's triumph.

Subjects: blind, books and reading, Braille, elementary school, gifted and talented, learning disabled, physically handicapped, teachers

118   Metzger, Lois. *Barry's Sister*. Atheneum. 1992. Hardcover 227pp. Ages: 12 and up. ISBN: 0–689–31521–X $15.95.

This sensitive and informative novel spans three years in Ellen Gray's life. At age twelve Ellen learns that her mother is pregnant, and she wishes the baby would disappear. When her brother, Barry, is born with cerebral palsy, she feels she is responsible due to her wish and suffers extreme guilt. She is also angry because her father, who is a naval officer on a nuclear submarine, is away most of the time. At first her guilt forces her to avoid Barry, but over time this changes and she becomes obsessively protective toward him. She practically takes over her mother's role, fights her father's efforts to care for Barry, and isolates herself from her friends and school. Equilibrium is restored when Ellen's mother and friend help Ellen achieve a more mindful outlook. At age fourteen she finds herself, a new best friend, fun, and a new closeness to her father. Ellen's narration focuses on Barry's disability and the realization that "he's a kid, a regular kid, and he wants you to like him, or hate him, or not care about him at all—anything but pity him." This account of a family's reaction to a child with cerebral palsy is told in natural, vivid language.

Subjects: cerebral palsy, physically handicapped, siblings

119 Metzger, Lois. *Ellen's Case*. Puffin Books. 1997. Paperback 189pp. Ages: 12 and up. ISBN: 0–14–038372–7 $4.99.

In this sequel to *Barry's Sister* (1992), Ellen, now age sixteen, describes the malpractice suit initiated by her parents against the doctor responsible for her four-year-old brother Barry's cerebral palsy. The trial is the focus of the story, and it is riveting. The suspense of the testimonies is powerful, and the medical information is detailed. Ellen's crush on Jack Frazier, the skillful, passionate attorney, adds interest to the drama of the three-week-long trial. Ellen gains a new perspective when she learns from the judge that the trial is for her protection when she will be Barry's guardian. It is not Barry's case. It's hers. The book ends with a positive verdict and the promise of a future relationship for Ellen with a young man who also has cerebral palsy. An understanding of cerebral palsy is presented through the thoughts, emotions, and actions of Ellen's family and friends.

Subjects: cerebral palsy, physically handicapped, siblings

120 Mikaelsen, Ben. *Petey*. Hyperion. 1998. Hardcover 280pp. Ages: 9 and up. ISBN: 0–7868–2376–3 $15.95.

Petey was born in Montana in 1920, with cerebral palsy. His parents try to take care of him, but after two years they reluctantly have to send him to live in a mental institution, where he is misdiagnosed as an idiot. Communicating with only facial expressions and crude sounds, Petey manages to touch several good-hearted caregivers with his zest for life. When he is eleven years old, he is moved to the institution's adult ward. Here he makes friends with a boy named Calvin, who is mildly retarded and has severe clubfeet. They form a lasting friendship that defies their disabilities. Petey grows up with a sharp intelligence, but he is locked in a twisted body. Many people come and go in Petey's grim existence. He experiences joy and love, sadness and loss, and struggle and triumph as strongly as anyone does. Years later, as old men, Petey and Calvin are separated. Petey is moved to a nursing home, where he comes into contact with a teenager named Trevor who protects him from some snowball-throwing bullies. At first Trevor is disgusted by Petey, but eventually they become more than friends. Trevor arranges Petey's reunion with Calvin, gets him a new wheelchair, and helps him discover the outside world. Trevor remains Petey's devoted companion through his final illness.

This touching story affirms the strength of the human spirit and the power of friendship and compassion. It promotes the need to treat all people with respect and dignity. Spanning over seventy-five years, the book is also a history of how people with disabilities have been treated in this country. It chronicles conditions that are unimaginable by today's standards, and it shows how public misunderstanding was and continues to be an obstacle faced by people with disabilities.

Subjects: bullies, cerebral palsy, healthcare facilities, historical fiction, intergenerational relationships, physically handicapped, wheelchairs

121 Mikaelsen, Ben. *Stranded.* Hyperion. 1995. Paperback 247pp. Ages: 9 and up. ISBN: 0-7868-1109-9 $4.95.

Riding the ocean waves on her dinghy is the only place twelve-year-old Koby Easton feels at home. Koby lost her right foot in a bicycle accident four years ago. She wears an artificial foot that she calls her leggy. In her watery world, she doesn't need two feet and there's nobody there to stare at her. Her parents are overprotective, and they argue a lot. Koby is convinced their fighting is because of her. At Lonesome Key Junior High, kids treat her as if she has a dreaded disease and act as if they would lose a foot, too, if they sat next to her. It's so unfair, and it hurts her. While navigating through the Florida Keys, Koby rescues an injured pilot whale and her calf that were stranded out on the sand flats. The Coast Guard takes the whales to a boat basin where they can be nursed back to health, but the whales are scared and don't respond. Koby is called in to calm them. The whales recognize her, relax, and allow the veterinarians to treat and feed them. In recognition of her brave actions, Koby is made an honorary member of the Lonesome Key Pod Squad volunteers. Never before has she felt so important. However, when her seventh-grade class comes to the basin on a field trip to see the whales, Koby becomes anxious and irritated because she doesn't want to share her special, private world. She panics when her classmates arrive and see her without her leggy. The veterinarian explains to them that the whales trust Koby. They don't see her as a person with a missing foot. By looking through with their sonar, they see something special inside Koby that makes her a friend. This is a lesson that everyone can learn from whales. Later, at school, through some interesting gym class activities, the kids learn more about Koby's disability. They start to understand, and Koby feels like a different person. This captivating adventure story about a daring and spunky girl who finds a way around her troubles and gains an improved self-image also offers facts about whales and the Florida Keys.

Subjects: boating, Florida, middle school, nature, physically handicapped, self-perception, sports

122   Millman, Isaac. *Moses Goes to a Concert.* Farrar, Straus & Giroux. 1998. Hardcover 32pp. Ages: 4–8. ISBN: 0–374–35067–1 $16.00. Illustrated by the author.

Moses and his classmates are deaf. They attend a young people's orchestral concert and reveal to readers that the ability to hear is not a prerequisite for enjoying music. The children feel the music as the balloons they hold on their laps pick up the vibrations. They are surprised when they discover that the percussionist wears no shoes. Mr. Samuels, their teacher, signs that the percussionist is deaf and that she follows the orchestra by feeling the vibrations of music through her stocking feet. After the concert Mr. Samuels takes the children onstage to meet the percussionist. Using American Sign Language, she explains that she became ill and lost her hearing at the age of seven. Her heart was set on becoming a percussionist, she worked hard, and she achieved her career goal. She lets Moses and his friends play the marimba, the triangle, the cymbal, various drums, bells, and the gong. On their bus ride back to school, Moses signs, "It was so much fun!" And that night he tells his parents, "When you set your mind to it, you can become anything you want when you grow up." The story is told in clear, colorful pictures, written in English, and precisely illustrated American Sign Language diagrams. An introductory note explains how to read the sign language illustrations, and the last page shows the hand alphabet. Readers can easily learn key words and ideas. This book deserves the waves and applause that Moses and his classmates offer. It is beautiful music.

Subjects: deaf, elementary school, music, physically handicapped, sign language

123   Millman, Isaac. *Moses Goes to School.* Farrar, Straus & Giroux. 2000. Hardcover 32pp. Ages: 4–8. ISBN: 0–374–35069–8 $16.00. Illustrated by the author.

Moses goes to a special public school for the deaf. It is the first day of school, and the children share their summer experiences: five baby hamsters, a cute new baby sister, new hearing aids, and new red glasses. They communicate in American Sign Language (ASL), visual signs, and facial expressions. In addition to science, arithmetic, and social studies, students learn ASL and how to read and write spoken English. They compose letters in ASL on paper, transfer them into English on computers, and then send them to their pen pals by electronic mail. Music is a very important part of their school day. Moses and his classmates don't hear the music, but they feel the vibrations when their teacher plays "Take Me Out to the Ball Game" on the boom box. They sign the song and make a circle and dance. Moses has ten classmates who come from many different countries. This diversity emphasizes that special-needs youngsters come from all cultures. The watercolor and ink cartoon illustrations show many details in the classroom and the fun the children have learning. Also included are small diagrams of Moses signing simple sentences. An author's note provides information about American Sign Language and explains how to follow the diagrams in the book to learn some words that are used throughout the story in ASL.

Subjects: deaf, elementary school, music, physically handicapped, sign language, special education

124 Mills, Claudia. *Lizzie at Last*. Farrar, Straus & Giroux. 2000. Hardcover 152pp. Ages: 9–12. ISBN: 0–374–34659–3 $16.00.

Twelve-year-old Lizzie Archer is too different. She is "off the scale for nerdiness." Classmates call her "The Lizard" or "The Brain." She writes poetry, is a math whiz, recites Shakespeare, and prefers long flouncy, romantic white dresses. Her parents are college professors, and Lizzie has spent her entire childhood in the company of adults or alone. Now starting seventh grade, she desperately wishes to be liked. She dons Gap jeans and tank tops, emulates the popular Marcia Faitak, attends roller skating parties and football games, and has an obvious crush on Ethan Winfield. She even deliberately turns in wrong answers in math, thinking that boys don't like brainy girls. Ethan, her math partner, is disappointed and angry when their math grade falls. But Lizzie is the most disappointed and confused. She is a new Lizzie on the outside, but she can't be a new Lizzie on the inside. To be happy, she knows that she has to follow her own star. So she decides to wear her Emily Dickinson dress to the dance. She does have true friends, is going to give her best to the Mathletes, and will write poems that might be in the university rare book room someday. The popularity and individuality concerns of middle schoolers are authentically explored in this charming story of Lizzie's newfound self-confidence.

Subjects: high school, popularity, self-perception

125 Mitchell, Lori. *Different Just Like Me*. Charlesbridge. 1999. Hardcover 32pp. Ages: 5–8. ISBN: 0–83106–915–2 $15.95. Illustrated by the author.

The author wrote this book when her young daughter who has vitiligo, a loss of pigment that presents itself as white spots all over the skin, started to look different from her classmates and also began to notice differences in others. The book explains how we are all different in some ways and alike at the same time. The story is told from the point of view of a little girl anticipating a visit to her grandmother, but she has to wait a whole week. On Monday, on the bus to town they encounter a girl who is hearing impaired and uses sign language. This page is bordered with the Gallaudet alphabet. On Tuesday, they go to the farmer's market and see people of all shapes, sizes, and colors. On Wednesday, at Dad's office they ride in the elevator with a blind woman. Braille numbers are included here. On Thursday, at the diner they meet a lady in a wheelchair. And on Friday, at the train station they see more differences—age, gender, and race. All these people are different but are doing the same things the little girl is. Finally they arrive at her grandmother's, and the young girl comes to realize that differences can be beautiful.

The detailed illustrations make this book especially appealing. In order to emphasize the diversity of colors in all people, all the background color is removed. The bright acrylic figures appear in black and white settings. The last pages at Grandmother's are in full color to reinforce the correlation between the beauty of the flowers and the beauty of all the different people.

Subjects: blind, Braille, deaf, grandparents, intergenerational relationships, physically handicapped, sign language, skin, wheelchairs

126 Moon, Nicola. *Lucy's Picture*. Dial Books. 1995. Hardcover 24pp. Ages: 4–8. ISBN: 0–8037–1833–0 $9.00. Illustrated by Alex Ayliffe.

Brightly colored children's artwork on the endpapers sets the stage for this joyous story. Lucy's grandpa is coming to visit. Today her class is going to do some painting. But painting isn't right for Lucy. She asks if she can "stick things on to make a picture." Her teacher lets her make a collage. She starts by plunging her hands into the scrapbox and "feeling with her eyes shut." She creates hills of soft green velvet, a lake of shiny blue, and flowers of dress material. At recess she collects twigs, leaves, feathers, and sand. She even snips a piece of her own hair for the dog in her picture. When her mom and grandpa arrive at school, it is revealed that grandpa is blind. He touches the picture carefully and exclaims, "It's the best picture I've ever seen." Lucy's imaginative picture is reproduced on one of the final pages. The torn-paper collages and the simple text will encourage young children to create their own textured collages and see in a different way.

Subjects: art, blind, elementary school, grandparents, intergenerational relationships, physically handicapped

127 Moran, George. *Imagine Me on a Sit-Ski!* Albert Whitman & Co. 1994. Hardcover 32pp. Ages: 5–10. ISBN: 0–8075–3618–0. Out of print. Illustrated by Nadine Bernard Wescott.

Billy, who has cerebral palsy and tells his story with a wordboard, is excited and scared about learning to ski. He explains the many different types of adaptive ski equipment that he and his physically challenged classmates use. He offers a lot of information about sit-ski technique. He shares all of his emotions. During his adventure his confidence grows, and in the end he is very proud of his achievement. He wonders what other sports he might be able to try. The bright watercolor illustrations and Billy's upbeat story will inspire and encourage understanding.

Subjects: cerebral palsy, physically handicapped, skiing, sports

128 Myers, Anna. *Ethan between Us.* Walker & Co. 1998. Hardcover 160pp. Ages: 12 and up. ISBN: 0–8027–8670–7 $15.95.

Fifteen-year-olds Clare and Liz have been best friends since kindergarten. But this changes when Ethan Bennington moves to their small Oklahoma oil town in July 1960. Ethan is good-looking, sensitive, and a gifted classical pianist. Clare is intelligent and an aspiring poet. While Liz is away for the summer, Clare grows close to Ethan. He reveals that he has been diagnosed as a schizophrenic and has spent time in a mental hospital because he hears the voice of a nineteenth-century composer who knew Brahms, died young, and wants his concerto written down. Clare is drawn deeper and deeper into the mystery of Ethan's life and music. When Liz returns for the start of school, Clare recognizes the strain on their relationship. Liz discovers Ethan's secret in Clare's diary, and feeling completely betrayed, she spreads the information around their high school. The book ends abruptly and tragically. The action of the story takes place in only ninety days, and the book ends with Clare's graduation speech in which she urges her classmates to "work for their dreams, to listen to life's music, and to appreciate people who are different." This teen romance with its complex characters and a hint of the supernatural is a compelling quick-read.

Subjects: emotional problems, high school, mentally ill, music, Oklahoma, schizophrenia

129 Newman, Leslea. *Fat Chance.* Putnam & Grossett Group. 1994. Paperback 214pp. Ages: 12 and up. ISBN: 0–698–11406–X $5.99.

Judi Liebowitz writes in her diary that she wants to be the thinnest girl in the eighth grade and that she wants Richard Weiss to be her boyfriend. She thinks she is fat and not pretty and not smart. She thinks she doesn't have a chance with Richard Weiss because fat girls don't deserve boyfriends. Judi becomes obsessed with losing weight. She likes to eat. When she baby-sits she has no willpower; she eats everything in the house: pretzels, potato chips, Tootsie Rolls, and ice cream, and she takes the wrappers home so no one will know. She tries to cut down on calories, but her mom prepares very fattening meals. Judi loses some weight by fasting and exercising, but her mom insists that she doesn't need to lose weight. Then she discovers a "secret weapon." Gorgeous Nancy Pratt, the most popular and thinnest girl in the eighth grade, eats too much and then throws up on purpose. Nancy explains that a lot of girls do it, especially models, actresses, and dancers. Yes, it's disgusting, but "not as disgusting as being fat." Judi starts doing it, too, considering that it's the "price of beauty." It becomes a secret that she hides from her mom and her friends. Diary entries tell Judi's whole story. She is teased and called Miss Piggy by Tommy Aristo. Richard Weiss asks her out but ends up dating her best friend, Monica. Her English teacher, and eventual confidante, is fat Ms. Roth, who used to be bulimic. She tells Judi that there are "more important things in life than a twenty-inch waist." Judi's relationship with her single-parent mom becomes very strained, and Judi gets more and more involved with Nancy Pratt. The girls "cover" each other's binge and purge cycles of bulimia. When she discovers Nancy passed out on the bathroom floor and Nancy is subsequently hospitalized, Judi realizes that she, too, has an eating disorder that is a matter of life and death. She lets her mom read her diary and agrees to see a therapist. The therapist will help Judi, and it's possible that she will end up with a body that she can really like. Judi's diary is serious yet humorous. It is inspirational reading for girls struggling with self-image and the enormous societal pressure to be thin.

Subjects: eating disorders, emotional problems, mentally ill, middle school, overweight, popularity, self-perception

130 O'Connell, Rebecca. *Myrtle of Willendorf*. Front Street. 2000. Hardcover 116pp. Ages: 12 and up. ISBN: 1–886910–52–9 $15.95.

It's the summer before Myrtle's sophomore year in college, but high school memories make up much of this story. Myrtle, who is seriously overweight, has a compulsive eating disorder. In high school she was best friends with Margie and a member of a coven that worshipped a robust, beautiful woman, the Venus of Willendorf. The coven also advocated self-affirmation and believed that each woman should embrace the goddess within her. Myrtle rejects her old friendship with Margie and moves on to college, new friends, and her roommate, Jada. Jada has a dancer's body, tries to recruit Myrtle into her world of slenderness and cosmetics, and along with her attractive boyfriend can be quite annoying. Myrtle, an aspiring artist, exhibits a shocking painting of Jada's boyfriend at Horton's Coffee Shop and Grill. Horton's has a Dr. Seuss motif, and its owner, Sam, adds an extra dash to the story. However, at the exhibit opening Myrtle overhears Jada's friends ridicule her. Myrtle's subsequent hate and anger precipitate her painting a self-portrait that she displays at Horton's. In so doing she discovers her own path, returns to her old friend Margie, and gains insight about her own beauty. The dialogue and characters are witty and provocative. There are many laugh-aloud scenes along the way to this unusual heroine's self-discovery. This coming-of-age story sends a clear message to young people struggling to find out who they are.

Subjects: art, eating disorders, emotional problems, high school, mentally ill, overweight, self-perception

131   Orr, Wendy. *Arabella.* Harper Collins. 1998. Hardcover 32pp. Ages: 4–8. ISBN: 0-207-19164-6 $16.00. Illustrated by Kim Gamble.

Matthew is spending the summer with his grandfather, who lives on an island and goes everywhere by boat. Grandpa's small crooked house is filled with his treasures. There are ships in glass bottles, the paddle from his first canoe, rainbow shells, driftwood, and a small perfect ship called the *Arabella*. Grandpa's grandpa built the ship, and now it sits in the window to bring him luck. Matthew uses a wheelchair, but that doesn't stop him from learning to sail. Grandpa tells stories of the sea and teaches Matthew to tie knots. One night a terrible storm smashes the window in Grandpa's house, and in the morning the *Arabella* is missing. Grandpa says it's no use. The ship is gone forever. But Matthew is determined to find the *Arabella*. He goes to the wharf and slides into Grandpa's boat. He spots the small ship bobbing in the rough sea and struggles to save the *Arabella*. Exhausted, he drifts back to the wharf, where worried Grandpa is waiting. Grandpa hugs Matthew tight, revealing that his greatest treasure is Matthew, not the *Arabella*. Matthew's disability is handled gently. It is never mentioned in the text. The watercolor paintings of the island and sea are enchanting.

Subjects: boating, grandparents, intergenerational relationships, physically handicapped, wheelchairs

132   O'Shaughnessy, Ellen. *Somebody Called Me a Retard Today . . . and My Heart Felt Sad.* Walker and Co. 1992. Hardcover 18pp. Ages: 4–8. ISBN: 0-8027-8197-7 $15.85. Illustrated by David Garner.

The simple and sensitive language of this story confirms the strengths of a young girl who is hurt when someone calls her a "retard." Her father reminds her that she is loving and determined and that she has feelings just like other kids do. The message that words can hurt can be easily understood through the clear text and soft watercolor illustrations.

Subjects: elementary school, mentally handicapped

133   Osofsky, Audrey. *My Buddy.* Henry Holt & Co. 1992. Hardcover 32pp. Ages: 5–8. ISBN: 0-8050-1747-X $15.95. Illustrated by Ted Rand.

This is the story of a boy with muscular dystrophy and Buddy, his service dog. They go through a tough training camp where they practice commands, sleep and even shower together, and learn to trust each other. After they graduate the boy and his golden retriever are a team. They shop, go to school, and play wiffle ball. Buddy helps the boy do things he couldn't do by himself, like turning on a light switch or answering the phone. The book is not about muscular dystrophy, but about the boy's desire to be independent and treated like everyone else. Even more important, it is about the team's wonderful friendship. It is realistic about the seriousness of what working dogs do and how important they are. Upbeat first-person prose and cheery watercolor illustrations emphasize the closeness between the boy and his dog.

Subjects: dogs—service, elementary school, muscular dystrophy, physically handicapped, service dogs, wheelchairs

134   Park, Barbara. *Dear God, Help!!! Love, Earl* (Geek Chronicles #3). Random House. 1993. Paperback 125pp. Ages: 9–12. ISBN: 0-679-85395-2 $4.50.

Three oddball students are best friends in their fifth-grade class. Earl Wilber is overweight, has a cowlick, and is allergic to grass. He is a funny and peace-loving boy. He is constantly pestered by Eddie McFee, a mean bully who calls Earl "Tubs" or "Jumbo." Earl pays Eddie two dollars a week to keep Eddie from beating him up. Earl's best friends are snoopy Rosie Swanson, who is a geek and a snitch, and scrawny Maxi Ruckerman, who is the biggest brain in the school. The three come up with an ingenious plan for seeking revenge against Eddie. With posed photos of Earl and a dog cemetery, they convince Eddie that he has actually killed Earl. Eddie cries, and then they tell him the truth. They threaten blackmail but agree not to tell the world about Eddie's tears if he agrees to choose Earl and Maxie first for teams in gym class. Earl does some deep thinking for a fifth grader. He does not get depressed. Even with his faults of being overweight and lacking self-confidence, he would rather be himself than a jerk like Eddie McFee. He builds courage and a "magical new feeling of self-confidence." In the end, he is "just a regular kid with a little bit of a weight problem and two amazing friends." This bright story is the third book in the Geek Chronicles trilogy.

Subjects: bullies, elementary school, overweight, popularity, self-perception

135 Parr, Todd. *It's Okay to Be Different.* Little, Brown. 2001. Hardcover 32pp. Ages: 4–8. ISBN: 0–316–66603–3 $14.95. Illustrated by the author.

Bright colors and simple drawings deliver the message that differences are okay. "You are special and important just because of being who you are." "It's okay to need some help" features a smiling blind girl with a yellow guide dog. "It's okay to have BIG ears" pictures a yellow rabbit with blue ears. A child in a purple wheelchair illustrates "It's okay to have wheels." Other differences depicted are size, wearing glasses, missing teeth, having a pet worm, and being adopted. This cheery picture book focuses on acceptance, individuality, and self-esteem.

Subjects: adoption, blind, dogs—service, physically handicapped, self-perception, service dogs, wheelchairs

136 Paterson, Katherine. *Flip-Flop Girl.* Lodestar Books. 1994. Hardcover 120pp. Ages: 8–12. ISBN: 0–525–67480–2 $13.99.

Grieving her father's death, nine-year-old Vinnie, her five-year-old brother, Mason, and their mother move to a small Virginia town to live with her grandmother. It's been three months since the evening at the funeral home when Vinnie's cruel words caused Mason to stop speaking. Vinnie resents that everyone's attention goes to Mason because of his "great reputation for the saddest boy that ever lived." At first she hates Brownsville, where everything is brown and gray. She doesn't want to go to fourth grade at Gertrude B. Spitzer Elementary School, where the girls wear pretty new jeans and the right brand of sneakers. She has to watch out for Mason, who attends kindergarten there. She thinks he should be in "a special school for troubled children—or troubling children—or children who were nothing but trouble." And no one can take her best friend Shawna's place. However, Vinnie is fascinated by one girl, Lupe, who wears orange flip-flops and is also an outsider, like herself. Vinnie's teacher, Mr. Clayton, is sensitive to her troubles and comforts her. He encourages her poetry writing and gives her red barrettes to keep her unruly hair out of her eyes. But Vinnie becomes jealous when Mr. Clayton gives a pair of shoes to Lupe and, worst of all, gets married. In her anger and confusion, she vandalizes his car and lets Lupe take the blame. In her agony she once again is cruel to Mason. She tells him she never wants to see him again, and he runs away. Suspense builds as Lupe helps rescue Mason when they find him on the dangerous railroad trestle. Mason finally speaks, and his words are heartbreaking. This powerful, easy-to-read story reveals insight into grief, rivalry, forgiveness, and resiliency, all sensitive issues for children.

Subjects: death, elective mutism, elementary school, grief, siblings

137 Patterson, Nancy Ruth. *The Shiniest Rock of All*. Farrar, Straus & Giroux. 1994. Paperback 72pp. Ages: 4–8. ISBN: 0–374–46615–7 $4.95. Illustrated by Karen A. Jerome.

Robert Morris Reynolds is a likable fourth grader who is full of mischief and who hates his name because he can't say his r's correctly. His older sister and his classmates constantly tease him. He doesn't want them to know that his speech problem bothers him. His distress causes him to retaliate, and he never gets away with much. He really gets into trouble when he smashes his peanut-butter-and-jelly sandwich into Ashley Allston's face. Robert's parents and teachers encourage him to see Miss Cooper, a speech therapist. She promises him a special, shiny rock when he can pronounce *rock* correctly. As Robert confronts his speech difficulty, he gains confidence and learns to be more understanding of others. Natural fourth graders' conversation, the fast-moving plot, and simple black and white illustrations of Robert's exploits will appeal to young readers.

Subjects: elementary school, physically handicapped, speech disorders, teachers

138 Paulsen, Gary. *The Monument*. Delacorte Press. 1991. Hardcover 151pp. Ages: 12 and up. ISBN: 0–385–30518–4 $15.00.

Rachel (Rocky) Turner is thirteen years old and was adopted by kind Emma and Fred Hemesvedt of Bolton, Kansas, when she was nine. She didn't think she would ever be adopted because her skin is the color of caramel and her left leg is deformed and braced. It's in her head that she can't be pretty with a bad leg. Kids tease her because they think her leg is funny, but mostly they just leave her alone. Her best friend is her devoted dog, Python. Then Mick Strum comes to town. He is an untamed artist who is commissioned by Rocky's small Kansas town to create a monument to honor their eighteen war dead. Mick is rough and likes to drink, but he has a keen artist's eye. Through his sketching, he gets a feel for the townspeople. At first they don't like what they see in his drawings. But in just three days he convinces them that the most meaningful monument will be a grove of trees where people can sit in the quiet shade and think of what the trees represent. More important, he changes Rocky's view of life and art. In learning to really observe, she discovers herself and her own desire to be an artist.

Subjects: adoption, art, physically handicapped

139   Peters, Julie Anne. *How Do You Spell Geek?* Little, Brown. 1996. Hardcover 139pp. Ages: 8–12. ISBN: 0–316–70266–8 $12.95.

Best friends Kimberly and Ann are eighth graders who practice day and night for the National Spelling Bee in Washington, D.C. Ann is assigned to sponsor a new student, Lurlene Brueggemeyer. Lurlene is a "creepy creature with braces" who wears pink bows in her hair, a corduroy jumper over a checkered flannel shirt, and cowboy boots. She is a "galactic geek." Ann is embarrassed to be seen with her, and people are starting to talk. Lurlene was home schooled before coming to Shiffley Middle School. She is very bright and a dynamite speller. Ann helps the misfit girl with her appearance. Lurlene gets her hair styled and new clothes and is quite happy that Ann "degeeked" her. Ann explains that "clothes aren't important to who you are inside, but . . . a lot of people don't look any further." Ann and Lurlene become good friends, and Kimberly feels threatened. The three girls end up competing against each other at the state spelling competition. Kimberly is eliminated in round three. Lurlene and Ann make it to the final round, which is a spell-down between the two of them that continues until Lurlene misses *psaltery* and Ann wins with *onchocerciasis*. Kimberly and Lurlene congratulate Ann, the new Colorado state finalist, and offer to help her prepare for nationals. This energetic novel explores middle-school concerns of fitting in, popularity, and friendship. Ann is a strong and compassionate character who becomes a better person by befriending and helping the geeky Lurlene.

Subjects: middle school, popularity, self-perception

140 Piper, Deb. *Jake's the Name, Sixth Grade's the Game*. Royal Fireworks Press. 1996. Paperback 62pp. Ages: 9–12. ISBN: 0-88092-135-8 $9.99.

Sixth grader Jake Zulinski introduces himself as brainy, witty, and good looking. He is inquisitive and has a dynamic personality. He is also deaf. Sometimes his deafness makes a difference, but mostly he's like everyone else. He can be just as mischievous or angelic as anyone. Jake's humorous first-person account of his entire school year at Lincoln Elementary School tells what it's like to be mainstreamed into the sixth grade of a public school. He explains about interpreters, teachers wearing microphones, and closed captioners. He describes sign language class, where his classmates learn how to sign. They particularly enjoy signing songs. Some of the kids are so skilled in sign language that they use it to help each other on tests, with some funny results. Jake relates how he "feels" music and even square dances in gym class. He discovers that square dancing is a way to drive girls crazy. And he offers an amusing story about how his interpreter sometimes signs things completely different from what the teacher is saying when she knows Jake isn't paying attention. One day in health class, she signs "The Twelve Days of Christmas" instead of the information about cells. The school year ends with Jake's graduation ceremony, where the whole class signs "Come to America." It makes him feel good that the kids are so comfortable signing, and it makes him feel more a part of the class. Light-hearted and informative, Jake's story is important for adolescents in mainstreamed classrooms in public schools, as well as their parents. Teachers and others professionally involved with deaf students will also benefit from this enjoyable book written by an interpreter. A sequel, *The Sevy Blues*, chronicles the seventh-grade adventures of feisty Jake.

Subjects: deaf, elementary school, middle school, music, physically handicapped, sign language, teachers

141 Plum-Ucci, Carol. *The Body of Christopher Creed*. Harcourt, Inc. 2000. Hardcover 256pp. Ages: 12 and up. ISBN: 1-15-202388-7 $17.00.

When Chris Creed, the class outsider, mysteriously vanishes, rumors fly in the town of Steepleton. In an enigmatic e-mail message left by Chris twenty-four hours before he disappeared, he describes his envy of Torey Adams and some of his friends who are their high school's star athletes with beautiful girlfriends. Chris ends the message by stating that he wants to "be gone." Is it a murder, suicide, abduction, or runaway? Sixteen-year-old Torey is haunted by Chris's disappearance, and in searching for answers he discovers that people are not always what they appear to be. He develops compassion toward those who are different. He gets to know some of the town misfits, like Ali and Bo. Ali is a childhood schoolmate with a reputation for sleeping around who turns out to be a trustworthy friend. And Bo is an outcast "boon" from the boondocks edge of town with a long juvenile record and a surprising caring streak. The three set forth to solve the mystery by trying to steal Chris's diary in the hopes of finding evidence, but they only succeed in implicating themselves. The body of Christopher Creed is never found, dead or alive. And although Chris never really appears in the novel, readers come to know how he felt as an outcast. Torey's narration takes place a year later from the boarding school he attends, during which time he is searching through the Internet for the missing Chris Creed. This fast-paced story offers mystery, plot twists, and an eye-opening look at alienation, cruelty, understanding, and loyalty.

Subjects: emotional problems, high school, mystery

142   Polacco, Patricia. *Thank You, Mr. Falker.* Philomel. 1998. Hardcover 40pp. Ages: 5–10. ISBN: 0–399–23166–8 $16.99. Illustrated by the author.

Children's author Patricia Polacco was once little Trisha, who in first grade loves books and drawing and desperately wants to learn to read. But when she looks at a page, the letters are wiggling shapes. When she tries to sound out words, kids laugh and her teacher moves on to the next child. Trisha begins to feel "different." To her, reading is torture. She thinks she is dumb. Kids tease her more and she hates school more. In fifth grade a new teacher, Mr. Falker, acknowledges her brilliant drawings and encourages her artwork. He realizes that Trisha is dyslexic. She doesn't see letters or numbers the way other people do. Every day, for months, she works with Mr. Falker and Miss Plessy, a reading teacher, and finally the words and sentences take shape and she understands what she reads. Trisha starts to love school and the "odyssey of discovery and adventure." Colorful gouache and pencil illustrations capture the essence of reaching a struggling student. This autobiographical tale is a thank-you to teachers who appreciate children's strengths, help them overcome reading disabilities, and consequently change lives.

Subjects: art, books and reading, dyslexia, elementary school, learning disabled, teachers

143   Powell, Randy. *Tribute to Another Dead Rock Star.* Farrar, Straus & Giroux. 1999. Hardcover 215pp. Ages: 12 and up. ISBN: 0–374–37748–0 $17.00.

Three years ago Debbie Grennan, a famous rock star, died after overdosing on drugs and alcohol. Her fifteen-year-old son, Grady, has been invited to Seattle to speak at a tribute concert for her. Grady needs a home. His grandmother, with whom he has been staying, has remarried and is taking off with her new husband to travel around the country in an RV (recreational vehicle). Boarding school in Europe scares Grady too much. And becoming a stage manager for a rock band has limited appeal. While in Seattle, Grady stays with Mitch, his architect father; Vickie, Mitch's staunch Christian wife; their three children; and Louis, Grady's twelve-year-old half-brother who is mentally retarded. Louie drains, exhausts, and frustrates Grady. People notice Louie because of his grin, his vacant stare, and his rocking movements. People notice Grady when Louie is with him, and Grady does not like to be noticed. However, Grady loves his brother. He doesn't like the boys who pester Louie and call him "ree-tar-do." Grady has problems with Vickie, too. They clash on everything, especially on what's best for Louie. And another problem is the fact that Grady doesn't know what to say about his mother at the tribute concert. He feels that she cared about him but abandoned him because she cared more about her music. Grady spends three tense days with Mitch, Vickie, and Louie, but he experiences a form of acceptance from them and comes to terms with his mother's successes and failures. He finds his place and the family he's always wanted. Serious issues and references to rock music and skateboarding are intermingled in this first-person narration about a teen, his mentally retarded brother, and his unusual parents.

Subjects: high school, mentally handicapped, music, siblings

144 Pulver, Robin. *Way to Go, Alex!* Albert Whitman and Co. 1999. Hardcover 32pp. Ages: 5–8. ISBN: 0–8075–1583–3 $14.95. Illustrated by Elizabeth Wolf.

A note from the Special Olympics organization starts off Carly's positive story about her brother's participation in the Special Olympics. She is puzzled, frustrated, and ashamed because Alex's brain doesn't work right. Their mom signs Alex up for the fifty-meter dash, the softball throwing contest, and the standing long jump. Because they only have eight weeks to get ready, Carly decides to practice every day with Alex. On the day of the event, Carly cheers for Alex and feels the excitement of all the smiling contestants. Alex runs the fifty-meter dash but stops short of the finish line, thinking the ribbon means he should stop. He didn't understand because they hadn't practiced with a ribbon. He gets a third place medal in the event and also in the softball-throw. He earns a participant medal in the standing long jump. Carly isn't so happy with this until she realizes that Alex made everyone else happy by doing the best he could and by having the courage to try, and that she had helped. The story accurately tells how difficult it is to cope with a sibling's disabilities. The soft illustrations reflect the pride in the achievements of the special athletes.

Subjects: mentally handicapped, siblings, Special Olympics, sports

145 Quigley, James. *Johnny Germ Head*. A Redfeather Book, Henry Holt. 1997. Hardcover 72pp. Ages: 5–8. ISBN: 0–8050–5395–6 $14.95. Illustrated by JoAnn Adinolfi.

Johnny Jarvis's third-grade friends call him Johnny Germ Head because he is obsessed with germs. It started when his parents gave him a microscope when he was seven years old. He is afraid of the invisible enemies in the swimming pool at Kraft Kamp. He creates a germ battlefield out of clay. Kids tease him when he picks at his dinner of limp, soggy vegetables that look like dead bugs. Johnny takes a million showers to combat athlete's foot and poison sumac. And on the Sea Serpent roller coaster, he holds on to the safety bar with paper towels because it's worse than a doorknob that gets touched by hundreds of unwashed hands every day. This really embarrasses his friends. While on the roller coaster, he notices a toddler about to jump into the mucky moat under the track. When the ride stops, Johnny tears out of his seat and rescues the little boy from the germ-infested water. The crowd cheers, and the paramedics give Johnny antibiotics because he swallowed some dirty water. He wins his battle against germs. He figures he's pretty safe and that it's a lot better to worry about people who are in trouble than to worry about germs. Wacky black and white cartoons of germs add fun to this strange story of a young boy's obsessions and phobias.

Subjects: elementary school, obsessive-compulsive disorder

146 Quinn, Patrick. *Matthew Pinkowski's Special Summer*. Eagle Creek Publications. 1991. Paperback 188pp. Ages: 9–12. ISBN: 0–9645048–1–2. Out of print.

Reading and writing aren't easy for thirteen-year-old Matthew Pinkowski. At school he is in a special program that both embarrasses and angers him. He reads words slowly, can't remember what he just read, and consequently doesn't enjoy reading. He likes summer best because in the summertime he feels "just as smart as anybody and sometimes smarter." This special summer, in his new hometown, Stillwater, Minnesota, Matthew has one exciting adventure after another. First, he saves Tommy's life by dumping a wheelbarrow full of firewood into the street to stop a runaway station wagon. He is then honored as the hero of the year in the annual Pioneer Days parade. He becomes close friends with Tommy and Tommy's sister, Sandy. Tommy, too, is in special education classes. He wears thick glasses and learns, walks, and talks differently. But he has an unbelievable memory and is one of the friendliest kids Matthew knows. Matthew, Sandy, and Tommy explore secret caves on the cliffs of the St. Croix River. They meet Laura, who is visiting her aunt and uncle for a few weeks while her parents are in Europe. Laura is deaf. At first she lip-reads and writes notes in the dirt to communicate. She has hearing aids but doesn't like to wear them. She teaches her new friends how to fingerspell and then how to sign. Matthew finds that it's easier to spell with his hands than with a pencil. They spend three to four hours a day learning. And before long they understand each other pretty well. In telling about another summer adventure, Matthew relates how they figure out a tricky plan for a poker game with some older bullies. In the next adventure, Matthew and his friends look through a telescope and learn about astronomy from old man Jenkins, who also encourages them to read books and ask questions. He tells them, "There's so much to learn and you can learn it all." And in the ultimate adventure, the kids find out who is stealing boats from the river marina. When the first day of junior high comes, Matthew is almost glad to be back at school. His special summer has made him ready. The author of this brisk, often sophisticated, and funny narrative is a communication disorder specialist who works with middle-school special education students.

Subjects: bullies, deaf, learning disabled, middle school, Minnesota, physically handicapped, sign language

147 Radin, Ruth Yaffe. *Carver.* MacMillan. 1990. Hardcover 70pp. Ages: 9–12. ISBN: 0–02–775651–3. Out of print. Illustrated by Karl W. Swanson.

Ten-year-old Jon became blind eight years ago in a car accident that killed his father. He attended a special school near Washington, D.C., but now attends sixth grade in a public school in his new hometown, Kellam's Landing. He struggles to fit in at his new school, where he is the only blind student. He has to learn to type because he can't turn in Braille to a sighted teacher. And the teacher openly states that she doesn't want Jon in her classroom. She seats him off to the side so he won't distract the rest of the class with his special materials. Jon's mother assures him that once the teacher sees that Jon can do whatever the other kids can do for schoolwork, everything will be fine. Jon gets along with his new classmates and becomes good friends with Matt. Jon's dream is to carve wooden shore birds, like his father did, but he has to hide his interest in wood carving from his mother, who still mourns the death of his father. Matt knows the best local sculptor, a man known as Carver. The boys figure out a way for Jon to meet Carver and hope that Carver will teach Jon. Carver is a gruff man and a recluse. Jon must convince him that a blind boy can carve. Jon is determined, and Carver does believe in him and his "good hands." He uses some different teaching techniques to get Jon to feel shapes. Jon eventually carves a duck that is better than some done by grown-ups. He shows his mother, hoping that if she sees what he can do, she will approve of his carving. She calls the duck beautiful, is proud of Jon, and realizes that his woodcarving brings back good memories. This short novel was inspired by Curtis Merritt, a blind wood carver who believed that "the only real handicap a blind person has is the people who think he can't do anything at all."

Subjects: birds, blind, grief, middle school, physically handicapped, teachers

148 Randle, Kristen D. *The Only Alien on the Planet*. Scholastic. 1995. Hardcover 228pp. Ages: 12 and up. ISBN: 0–590–46309–8 $14.95.

High school senior Ginny Christianson has just moved to town and is anxious to make new friends. Honor student Smitty Tibbs catches her attention. Smitty never speaks, smiles, or cries. He doesn't react, "like he's not aware there's anybody else in the universe." He is tolerated at school, and the kids pretty much leave him alone. Fellow student Caulder Pretiger befriends Ginny, and together they decide to try to break through Smitty's shell and bring him back into the world. They begin by going to Smitty's house for help with math. Then they start walking to school together, and eventually they attend movies at the Friday night film society at the university. Smitty still does not speak, but he does show some faint signs of responding to Ginny. Caulder explains to Ginny that Smitty hasn't talked since, at age two, his brother Russell tried to drown him. Ginny and Caulder try hard to break the barriers and communicate with Smitty, but they make some terrible mistakes. Smitty finally speaks his first words after Ginny kisses him. However, Smitty is hospitalized. It is his choice. With the help of a conscientious and sympathetic psychologist, Ginny and Caulder learn more of how Russell abused Smitty and convinced him that he would die if he spoke to anyone. Smitty's tough-mindedness, therapy, and medication, and his relationship with Ginny and Caulder, which grows because of their daily visits, help Smitty see hope and possibilities. This compelling novel that deals with sibling abuse and its resulting protective silence leaves a powerful impact.

Subjects: abuse, elective mutism, emotional problems, healthcare facilities, high school, mentally ill

149   Rau, Dana Meachen. *The Secret Code*. Children's Press. 1998. Hardcover 32pp. Ages: 5–8. ISBN: 0–516–20700–8 $18.00. Illustrated by Bari Weissman.

Oscar, who is blind, explains to his elementary school classmates that his books are written in Braille, not a secret code. He teaches them that Braille is a different way of reading. Oscar's friends read with their eyes. Oscar reads with his fingers. Either way, reading is fun. The Braille alphabet is illustrated. (It is disappointing that it is not printed as raised bumps, but the author does suggest that readers check their libraries for a Braille book that they can feel on their own.) The simple language and peppy watercolor-and-ink classroom scenes will help youngsters understand about children who are blind or visually impaired.

Subjects: blind, books and reading, Braille, elementary school, physically handicapped, visually handicapped

150   Richardson, Bill. *After Hamelin*. Annick Press, Ltd. 2000. Hardcover 227pp. Ages: 9–12. ISBN: 1–55037–629–2 $19.95.

This imaginative tale continues Robert Browning's poem "The Pied Piper of Hamelin." Penelope wakes up mysteriously deaf on her eleventh birthday. On the same day the Pied Piper returns to Hamelin to claim its children in an evil act of revenge. The Pied Piper plays his pipe and enchants the children with his bewitching tune, just as he did the rats. Only two children are spared. They are each protected by a disability. Penelope, because of her deafness, can't hear the Piper's entrancing melody; and Alloway, because of his blindness, is lost in the forest after the Piper's music finally fades away. In Hamelin, on every girl's eleventh birthday, old Cuthbert, the sage and seer of gifts, reveals from the Elevening Scrolls what her special gift will be. Penelope receives the unusual gift of deep dreaming. Cuthbert explains that her deafness is a gift. Because of it she escaped the Piper's snare, and because of it she holds the power to find and save the children of Hamelin. Armed with a necklace braided from eight harp strings, which Cuthbert gives to her, and her own courage, Penelope enters the land of sleep on a dangerous mission to save the lost children. She teams up with colorful companions along the way. There's Scally, her trusted talking cat; Alloway, the blind harpist; Belle, a singing, featherless Trolavian snowbird; Ulysses, a three-legged dog; and Quentin, a rope-skipping dragon. They travel over the hills and far away through strange landscapes to the Piper's fortress, which is a place between dreaming and waking. They triumph and renew the spell that will keep the Piper asleep and harmless and set the children free. Penelope, who is now 101 years old, narrates the lively and thoughtful fantasy. She hears "in a way that those who have only ears will never know." The story moves back and forth from the past to the present to the world of dreaming and is enhanced with creative wordplay, rope rhymes, and songs.

Subjects: blind, deaf, Germany, historical fiction, legend, music, physically handicapped

151   Rickert, Janet Elizabeth. *Russ and the Apple Tree Surprise*. Woodbine House. 1999. Hardcover 28pp. Ages: 4–8. ISBN: 1–890627–16–X $14.95. Photographs by Pete McGahan.

Five-year-old Russ has Down syndrome, but he is just an ordinary boy who likes apple trees and surprises. In a story told in simple language and charming photos, Russ's Daddy and Grandpa help Russ pick a basket of apples and then he helps his Mommy and Grandma bake a delicious apple pie. After dessert, Grandpa tells Russ that there's a big surprise outside in the backyard especially for him. He runs outside to discover a swing in the apple tree. Down syndrome is not mentioned in the text. This is the first book in the "A Day with Russ" series, written by a nurse who is a member of the National Association for Down Syndrome.

Subjects: Down syndrome, grandparents, intergenerational relationships, mentally handicapped

152   Rodowsky, Colby. *Clay*. Farrar, Straus & Giroux. 2001. Hardcover 166pp. Ages: 8–12. ISBN: 0–374–31338–5 $16.00.

Elsie McPhee, age eleven, and her autistic seven-year-old brother, Tommy, move from one anonymous town to another with their mother. They are not allowed to go to school and are forbidden to leave their apartment or talk to strangers. Tommy is withdrawn and doesn't talk much anyway. He spends most of his time swirling the stones he collects and stores in a red Folgers coffee can. Elsie takes care of Tommy because their mother works as a waitress to support their isolated and lonely lifestyle. Elsie begins to question her mother's rules and judgment when she realizes that they move and change their names whenever she makes a friend or when someone starts to ask questions. Elsie remembers the events of four years ago when their mother abducted her and Tommy, who were in the sole custody of their father. She also remembers that disagreements over Tommy being "different" and their mother's refusal to seek help for him led to their parents' divorce. When Tommy suddenly becomes ill while their mother is at work, Elsie takes serious risks to get help for her brother and herself. The siblings are finally rescued and reunited with their father. The tough readjustment begins as they return to their former life and come to grips with Tommy's autism and their mother's instability. Elsie's first-person account focuses on her devotion to Tommy and the confusion and frustration of being a kidnapped child. This moving story will keep readers on the edge of their seats.

Subjects: autism, siblings

153 Rodriguez, Bobbie. *Sarah's Sleepover.* Viking. 2000. Hardcover 32pp. Ages: 4–8. ISBN: 0–670–87750–6 $15.99. Illustrated by Mark Graham.

Sarah is blind, although the text does not specifically mention the fact. She can always hear cars before anyone else does. She knows her cousins by their footsteps. But she can't play checkers because she can't see the game board. Sarah and her cousins are all set for a sleepover. Amid hot chocolate and pillow fights, a storm causes the lights to go out. The girls, except Sarah, are scared. Sarah is comfortable moving in the dark. She guides her cousins downstairs to the telephone to call her parents, who are visiting neighbors. She knows the number by heart. She calms the girls by identifying frightening noises. When Sarah's parents return and the lights go on, the girls decide to stay in the dark and play guessing games and tell ghost stories. The cousins' emotional reaction to darkness compared to Sarah's is a thought-inspiring notion. Impressionistic paintings that are sensitive to light and dark illustrate this story about how a young girl's differences can sometimes be her greatest strength.

Subjects: blind, physically handicapped

154 Roos, Stephen. *The Gypsies Never Came.* Simon & Schuster. 2001. Hardcover 117pp. Ages: 9–12. ISBN: 0–689–83147–1 $15.99.

Augie Knapp is a tough but emotionally hurt sixth grader who keeps his deformed hand in a glove. He lives with his mother, works after school as a dry cleaning delivery boy, and doesn't even know his father's name. He secretly collects other people's letters, report cards, receipts, and greeting cards and hides them in an old suitcase. Through them, he lives a pseudo-normal life. Augie yearns to be like his classmates, but when the mystical and much-too-old-for-sixth-grade Lydie Rose shows up in his class, she emphasizes his difference and tells of sympathetic gypsies who will come for him and show him how special he is. Though Augie finally does remove his glove, Lydie Rose's influence on Augie remains unconfirmed. Is Lydie Rose a gypsy? And do Augie's dreams come true? This sensitive novel very subtly demonstrates the dissimilarity between being different and being special.

Subjects: middle school, physically handicapped

155 Rottman, S. L. *Head above Water.* Peachtree Publishers. 1999. Hardcover 192pp. Ages: 12 and up. ISBN: 1–56145–185–1 $14.95.

High school junior Skye Johnson is training to qualify for the state swimming championships and studying hard to keep her grades up in hopes of earning a college scholarship. Because her divorced mother has to work two jobs, Skye has to take care of Sunny, her older brother who has Down syndrome. Sunny frustrates and challenges her. She also has a new boyfriend, Mike, and she lies to her mother in order to spend more time with him. Mike wants more from her than she is willing to give. Skye struggles hard to keep her head above water, and in meeting her responsibilities she discovers what is important in her life and that she and Sunny are very much alike. The final scene where Skye cheers for Sunny in the Special Olympics swim meet is sensitively written.

Subjects: Down syndrome, high school, mentally handicapped, siblings, Special Olympics, swimming

156 Rupert, Rona. *Straw Sense.* Simon & Schuster. 1993. Hardcover 32pp. Ages: 5–8. ISBN: 0–671–77047–0 $14.00. Illustrated by Mike Dooling.

In a South African village surrounded by strawberry fields, five-year-old Goolam-Habib does not speak. He lost his voice the night the forest burned down; "but there is nothing wrong with his head," according to his aunt. He is as bright as anyone else. On his way to the roadside stall to buy potatoes and tomatoes, he notices a shed with an open door. He steps inside to escape the rain and finds an old man making a straw scarecrow-doll. He returns the next day to help the old man stuff feathers into an ostrich-doll. They work together and eventually create not only the man-doll and the ostrich; but his wife with blue eyes, a blue nose, and a blue mouth; and their beautiful blue daughter riding a red bicycle. Goolam-Habib sees the happiness in the amusing scarecrow-doll family and in the old man. Their loneliness is gone and so is his. Goolam-Habib finds himself and regains his voice. The textured oil paintings effectively portray the village culture, the smiling scarecrow-doll family in the strawberry field, and Goolam-Habib's pride.

Subjects: elective mutism, intergenerational relationships, South Africa

157 Russo, Marisabina. *Alex Is My Friend.* Greenwillow. 1992. Hardcover 32pp. Ages: 5–8. ISBN: 0–688–10418–5. Out of print. Illustrated by the author.

The author tells this story of the friendship of two boys, which is based on the experiences of her son. Ben, who narrates, asks his mother why Alex is smaller, even though he is older than Ben is. She explains that he will always remain small, although she never says he is a dwarf. Alex has to have surgery on his back and stay in a wheelchair for a time after he returns to school. They continue to play games and tell jokes. Ben can run faster than Alex can, but it doesn't matter because they are such good friends. The brightly colored, framed gouache paintings are pleasant. The text is bordered with miniature paintings that extend the story.

Subjects: dwarfism, elementary school, physically handicapped, wheelchairs

158 Ryden, Hope. *Wild Horse Summer.* Random House. 1997. Paperback 154pp. Ages: 9–12. ISBN: 0–440–41548–9 $4.50. Illustrated by Paul Casale.

Horse lovers will enjoy this pleasant story about Alison, who spends the summer of her thirteenth birthday on the Wyoming ranch of her blind cousin, Kelly. Alison has doubts about the trip. First, because she's afraid of heights, she won't fly and therefore travels by train. Second, she thinks she'll be expected to spend the summer leading Kelly around. And finally, horses seem pretty high and they scare her. Gradually she conquers all of her fears. She becomes a riding companion for her blind cousin, who is capable and independent. The summer turns into a true adventure. Alison rescues Kelly's horse, who is spirited away by a wild stallion. She takes on responsibilities on the ranch and also meets Matt, a handsome neighbor. When the summer is over, she flies home to Chicago and can't wait to return to Wyoming next summer. Full-page, black and white drawings and much factual information about American mustangs add to this romantic horse story.

Subjects: blind, horses, physically handicapped, Wyoming

159 Shreve, Susan. *The Gift of the Girl Who Couldn't Hear*. William Morrow and Co. 1993. Paperback 79pp. Ages: 12 and up. ISBN: 0–688–11694-9 $4.95.

Normally bright, friendly, and happy-go-lucky Eliza Westfield has wanted to be Annie in the seventh-grade musical since she was in third grade. But now, at age thirteen, she has lost her self-confidence. She feels awkward, uncoordinated, and fat. She has become bad-tempered and no longer gets A's in school. She can't bring herself to audition, but her best friend, Lucy, who was born deaf, announces that she is going to try out for a singing role. Lucy reads lips and can speak well for a deaf person. However, she can't sing. Kids tease Lucy because she's different. Eliza's mother explains that "people are afraid of differences" and "they don't know how to behave around people who are not exactly like them." Eliza tries to teach Lucy how to sing, and in the process the girls learn about their strengths and weaknesses. Unknown to Eliza, Lucy writes Eliza's name on the audition sign-up sheet. This easy-to-read novel about bravery and limitations ends with Eliza getting the part of Annie and Lucy becoming stage manager.

Subjects: deaf, middle school, music, overweight, physically handicapped, self-perception, theatre

160 Shreve, Susan. *Joshua T. Bates Takes Charge*. Dell Yearling. 1993. Paperback 102pp. Ages: 8–12. ISBN: 0–679–87039-3 $4.99. Illustrated by Dan Andreasen.

Fifth grader Joshua T. Bates worries about failing math and playing baseball. But mostly he worries about fitting in. Since he flunked third grade, he has had trouble with Tommy Wilhelm and his gang of bullies, called the "NOs," or Nerds Out. The NOs target dorky kids. Their new victim is Sean O'Malley. Sean has just moved to Mirch Elementary School from New Jersey. He's short, has red hair, and carries a Mickey Mouse lunchbox. Their teacher asks Joshua to show Sean around the school. Sean wants Joshua to be his new best friend, but Joshua can think of nothing worse than being linked up with the geeky new boy. Tommy and the NOs persecute Sean. They trip him in the hall, pull his stool out from under him in art class, dump a lunch tray on his head, steal his lunchbox, and tie him up in the school equipment shed. When confronted by the principal about Sean's problems, Joshua can't decide whether to stick up for Sean and tell what he knows or to be quiet and save himself from Tommy and the feared Nerds Out gang. Joshua's dad advises him to take charge, and Joshua realizes that he's smart enough to make his own decisions. He denounces Tommy at a special assembly, and his classmates cheer. This light yet thoughtful story tells what it's like to be an outcast and how one boy handles bullies.

Subjects: bullies, elementary school, popularity

161 Shriver, Maria. *What's Wrong with Timmy?* Little, Brown. 2001. Hardcover 48pp. Ages: 5–8. ISBN: 0–316–23337–4 $14.95. Illustrated by Sandra Speidel.

Eight-year-old Kate and her mother visit the park and notice Timmy, a boy who looks and acts differently from other children. His face seems flat, his glasses sit crookedly, one foot turns in, and he walks with a slight limp. Curious Kate wonders "what's wrong with Timmy?" Kate's mother clearly and calmly explains that Timmy was born different and that he has special needs. He takes longer to learn, he can't walk or run so well, and he talks slowly. But he loves his family, goes to school, and in many ways is just like Kate. She tells Kate that Timmy is disabled and has what doctors call mental retardation or a developmental disability. Kate's mom takes her to meet Timmy. Kate is nervous, but her mom informs her that "Timmy isn't someone to be afraid of." Everyone laughs when Kate asks Timmy if he likes math. Timmy admits that kids call him "slow" and "dumb" and that he has a hard time learning. Timmy's mom reminds him to be strong. Kate announces to her friends that Timmy is her new friend and includes him in their basketball game. The kids play ball and talk about TV and school, and Kate and Timmy set a play date for tomorrow. That night, Kate wonders "why God makes life so hard for a kid like Timmy." The next morning, Kate's mom answers that "each of us is here on Earth for a reason . . . Timmy included." She encourages Kate to look at what Timmy can do, not at what he can't do. Kate concludes that she and Timmy are truly more alike than they are different and that there's "nothing at all" wrong with Timmy. Kids have a chance to think for themselves with this tender story. Carefully chosen words appear in bold, large type in the text and serve as captions for the soft pastel illustrations. The author's family founded and continues to support the Special Olympics. A list of organizations that can provide information on various disabilities in included. This title is also available in a Spanish language edition.

Subjects: elementary school, mentally handicapped, physically handicapped

162 Slepian, Jan. *Risk N' Roses*. Scholastic Inc. 1992. Paperback 176pp. Ages: 9 and up. ISBN: 0–590–45361–0. Out of print.

It's 1948, and eleven-year-old Skip is tired of being responsible for Angela, her mentally handicapped older sister. She desperately wants acceptance in her new Bronx neighborhood and the friendship of the daring and magnetic Jean Persico. To become a member of Jean's secret club, the Dares, each girl must meet a risky challenge designed by Jean. The challenges range from putting a cockroach in an ice cream sundae to shoplifting. Skip makes it into the club, but when Jean's dare for Angela involves being cruel to their elderly neighbor, Skip finds her true loyalties and her own personal strength. The characters are well drawn in this serious novel about group dynamics.

Subjects: intergenerational relationships, mentally handicapped, popularity, siblings

163 Smith, Mark. *Pay Attention, Slosh!* Albert Whitman & Co. 1997. Hardcover 54pp. Ages: 9–12. ISBN: 0–8075–6378–1 $11.95. Illustrated by Gail Piazza.

This beginning chapter book shows how eight-year-old Josh always causes disturbances at school and at home. He acts up, can't sit down, and has a hard time paying attention. It bothers him that kids call him Slosh. And time-outs make him feel terrible. But mostly he is angry with himself because he can't stay out of trouble. Josh is bright when it comes to math and computers. He is also the best soccer player in his class. Josh's teacher recommends to his parents that he see a special doctor, who explains that Josh has attention-deficit hyperactivity disorder. Josh, the doctor, his parents, and his teacher work together to help Josh remember to concentrate. Josh is moved to the front of his class, where he is not so easily distracted. A reward system is started, and he earns enough stickers by doing what he is supposed to do that he can trade them in for a baseball cap. Josh improves, but the doctor recommends medication that will help him even more. The medicine helps. Josh doesn't like having ADHD, but he feels better knowing there's a reason why he sometimes can't sit still or pay attention. As he learns to concentrate, he bothers people less and they even stop calling him Slosh. This insightful and helpful bibliotherapeutic story is illustrated with black and white pencil sketches.

Subjects: attention-deficit hyperactivity disorder, elementary school, learning disabled, teachers

164   Sones, Sonya. *Stop Pretending: What Happened When My Big Sister Went Crazy*. Harper Collins. 1999. Paperback 149pp. Ages: 12 and up. ISBN: 0–06–446218–8 $6.95.

In a story told in intense, short, free verse poems, twelve-year-old Cookie honestly describes her feelings, starting with her sister's mental breakdown on Christmas Eve. Nineteen-year-old Sister suddenly starts screaming, runs out the door to Midnight Mass wearing only a nightgown, and becomes a stranger to Cookie and her parents. She has to be hospitalized. Cookie is horrified when she visits her sister and finds her rocking on all fours. She is afraid her friends will find out and also that she, too, might lose her mind. The poems powerfully capture Cookie's despair and grief over what happens to her sister and family. They recall happier times before the breakdown, and they also explore normal teenage situations, such as school and the joy of a first boyfriend. Cookie discovers that life goes on, and the book ends on a hopeful note as Sister, after many months, begins to show signs of recovery. The poems are based on the real-life events of the author, whose older sister suffered a breakdown, was placed in a psychiatric ward, and was diagnosed as manic-depressive. In an author's note, support Web sites and phone numbers for organizations that can help with mental illness are provided.

Subjects: emotional problems, healthcare facilities, mentally ill, middle school, poetry, siblings

165   Spears, Britney, and Lynne Spears. *A Mother's Gift*. Delacorte Press. 2001. Hardcover 240pp. Ages: 12 and up. ISBN: 0–385–72953–7 $14.95.

Fourteen-year-old Holly Faye Lovell leaves small-town Biscay, Mississippi, on a full scholarship to attend the prestigious Haverty School of Music in Hattiesburg. Her loyal, sweetheart of a boyfriend, who is a car mechanic, secured the audition, which now will allow her to pursue her dream of a singing career. But Holly has to leave behind her seamstress mother, Wanda, with whom she has a special bond. Wanda would be "drop-dead gorgeous" except for the two-inch-wide crimson birthmark on the side of her face. The conspicuous birthmark makes people who don't know Wanda turn away, and it is the most embarrassing thing Holly can think of. At first, at Haverty, Holly, her wardrobe, and her small-town ways are targets for her wealthy, snobbish classmates. But Holly is accepted and makes new friends, and her career takes flight. Still, she is ashamed of Wanda and doesn't even invite her to Parents' Weekend. This makes Holly feel horrible and begin to really appreciate everything her mom has done for her. In the final scene Wanda reveals a long-hidden secret. Her birthmark is really a burn scar she received rescuing one-month-old Holly from the tragic Biscay fire that killed Holly's parents. To keep her from being placed in an orphanage, Wanda adopted Holly. So the scar is a special "birthmark" of the moment Wanda saved Holly's life and became a loving mother for her. Wanda states that everyone has to find ways to deal with personal obstacles and that struggling with her birthmark has made her change how she feels about herself and others. Holly then wonders how she could have been ashamed of Wanda and the birthmark that made her mom "the most beautiful woman in the world." This fast-paced story of a teen singing sensation and coming to terms with facial disfigurement is a must-read for Britney fans.

Subjects: adoption, birthmarks, facial disfiguration, high school, music

166 Springer, Nancy. *Colt.* Penguin Putnam. 1994. Paperback 128pp. Ages: 8–12. ISBN: 0–14–036480–3 $4.99.

Colt Vittorio, whose age is never given in the text and who has spina bifida, is enrolled in a Horseback Riding for the Handicapped program. He is extremely reluctant and scared at first. He hates being handicapped. He hates being in a wheelchair and having to wear braces. He rides a big Appaloosa, named Liverwurst, and soon learns that riding strengthens his muscles and gives him freedom and self-assurance. Colt lives with his mother, who marries Brad, a compassionate man with a teenage son and daughter Colt's age. A minor accident on Liverwurst is life threatening for Colt because of his disability, and his mother decides he can no longer ride. Colt becomes very depressed until Brad buys Bonita, a small, quiet, and safe Paso Fino. Because his family realizes that the rewards of his riding are worth the risks, he is allowed to ride again. Colt develops a passion for riding and living. He can now do something normal kids can do. Some facts about spina bifida are presented in this uplifting story about Colt's struggles and triumphs.

Subjects: horses, physically handicapped, spina bifida, wheelchairs

167   Stepanek, Mattie J. T. *Journey through Heartsongs*. VSP Books. 2001. Hardcover 80pp. Ages: 12 and up. ISBN: 1–893622–10–X $14.95.

Real-life poet and peacemaker Mattie is eleven years old and has a rare form of muscular dystrophy that has taken the lives of his three siblings. He has been writing poetry and stories since he was three. Among those he has inspired are Jimmy Carter, Jerry Lewis, Steven Spielberg, and Oprah Winfrey. In "Future Echo," he writes about loneliness and the time when he won't be able to swing anymore. In "Unanswered Question," he is angry, scared, and confused about his brother Jamie's death. "About Wishing" tells that wishing is for everyone. It brings optimism, hope, new ideas, and the touch of new life for our future. In "Grounded Lesson," Mattie advises people to enjoy life even if it is a challenge because it is also a treasure. And he ponders cures for his condition in "I Could . . . If They Would." If they find a cure while he's still a kid, he could travel the world and teach peace. He could live each day without pain and machines and "celebrate the biggest thank you of life ever." If they find a cure when he's in Heaven, he could be happy knowing he was part of the effort. His colorful and simple illustrations shine alongside his wise and beautiful poetry. Mattie has published another book of poems, *Heartsongs*. He is the Maryland State Goodwill Ambassador for the Muscular Dystrophy Association and has been invited to speak at conferences and on television. Mattie is also like all kids. He enjoys reading and collecting rocks, and he has a Black Belt in martial arts.

Subjects: death, muscular dystrophy, physically handicapped, poetry

168   Stine, R. L. *Into the Dark* (Fear Street series). Archway Paperback. 1997. Paperback 147pp. Ages: 12 and up. ISBN: 0–671–52966–8 $3.99.

In this scary but predictable story in the Fear Street series, the main character, Paulette Fox, is blind. She was born blind and is used to other people doubting her abilities. She doesn't feel handicapped. She gets around perfectly with her cane, and her other senses are much sharper than most people's. She falls in love with Brad Jones. He doesn't care that she's different. They even both play the piano. But according to rumors, Brad is bad news. Paulette's life is threatened several times by a mysterious young man who may be Brad. And Brad is wanted for committing robberies in another city. Paulette's friends are sure they see Brad rob Pete's Pizza and shoot one of their friends, but Paulette is sure he is innocent and that he would never hurt her. The sound of the robber's voice and his smell tell Paulette that Brad is not the robber. And Paulette is right. Brad has a twin brother, Ed, who is "disturbed" and has been jealous of Brad throughout his whole life. He wanted Paulette for his girlfriend. He has always made trouble for Brad. In a terrifying final scene, Paulette saves Brad's life and Ed falls down the stairs to his death. Paulette Fox is an independent character who uses her senses and doesn't let her blindness keep her from living a very full life.

Subjects: blind, emotional problems, mystery, physically handicapped, siblings, twins

169 Strom, Maria Diaz. *Rainbow Joe and Me*. Lee & Low Books. 1999. Hardcover 34pp. Ages: 5–8. ISBN: 1–880000–93–8 $15.95. Illustrated by the author.

Eloise is a young African American artist. She mixes colors and paints fantastic pictures of cool pink fish and wild purple monkeys. When she tells Rainbow Joe, who is blind, about her colors and her paintings, he says she has imagination. He also tells her that even though he can't see with his eyes like she can, he can see colors inside his head. He can make colors sing. At first she doesn't understand, but his vivid descriptions of colors help. Finally he shows how he mixes colors when he plays his saxophone. He blows red and yellow notes to make orange, and he blows blue, green, and violet notes to make a big beautiful rainbow. Through Rainbow Joe's music, Eloise finds a whole new way of seeing and listening. The bold and brightly colored acrylic paintings and the imaginative text celebrate the joy of their friendship and the importance of sensory differences and similarities in this vibrant story.

Subjects: African Americans, art, blind, music, physically handicapped

170 Stuve-Bodeen, Stephanie. *We'll Paint the Octopus Red*. Woodbine House. 1998. Hardcover 28pp. Ages: 4–8. ISBN: 1–890627–06–2 $14.95. Illustrated by Pam De Vito.

At first young Emma is not happy about having a new sibling. Soon she thinks of all the things she can do with the baby. They can feed the calves at Grandpa's farm. They can paint pictures at the art festival. And they can go on a photo safari to Africa, if they let their dad come along. There are a million things they can do. But when baby Isaac is born with Down syndrome, Dad has to explain that although it may take more time, help, and patience, Isaac will be able to do all of the million things they thought of. The simple text makes it easy for a child to understand the message of accepting and helping. Questions that children have asked about their brother or sister with Down syndrome are appended. Answers are written at a child's level. The ink and watercolor illustrations present warm, positive pictures about Down syndrome in this sensitive story for any child to read.

Subjects: art, Down syndrome, mentally handicapped, siblings

171 Tashjian, Janet. *Multiple Choice*. Henry Holt. 1999. Hardcover 186pp. Ages: 9–12. ISBN: 0–8050–6086–3 $16.95.

Fourteen-year-old Monica Devon concludes that she spends 98.762 percent of her time obsessing about and analyzing her life. She worries about saying and doing the wrong thing, wearing the wrong clothes, and the word she spelled wrong in the fifth-grade spelling bee. She even worries about two lopsided beanbag chairs and has to transfer some of the styrofoam ball filling from one to the other until they are equal. A gifted wordsmith and a perfectionist, she invents a game, Multiple Choice, to lesson her anxiety about decision making. By randomly choosing Scrabble letters, she performs an act that is either (A) normal, (B) silly, (C) mean, or (D) charitable. By taking the choice out of making a decision, whatever the letters dictate is correct. She believes she can't be wrong anymore. At first the game is fun and liberating. But then it gets out of control. Her obsession with the game won't let her stop. She has to wear her pajamas to school, give away her favorite kaleidoscope, and alienate her best friend. When choice C leads her to lock Justin, the preschooler she baby-sits, in his room and he jumps out the window, injuring his eye, she realizes she needs help. Caring adults, especially her counselor, Darcy, turn her tendency for self-analysis in more positive directions. She learns that she can be insightful and spontaneous and creative, too. Monica is a complex character, and her talent for anagrams and other wordplay adds great fun to this cleverly constructed first-person portrait of a teen with obsessive-compulsive disorder.

Subjects: emotional problems, mentally ill, middle school, obsessive-compulsive disorder, self-perception

172 Tashjian, Janet. *Tru Confessions*. Scholastic. 1999. Paperback 167pp. Ages: 9–12. ISBN: 0–590–96047–4 $4.99.

This is a fast-moving story about twelve-year-old Trudy Walker and her dreams of finding a cure for her developmentally delayed twin brother, Eddie, and having a career in television, either in front of or behind the camera. It is creatively written in the form of an electronic diary, with frequent lists and questions, imaginative fonts, and computer graphics. Tru describes her work filming a documentary about Eddie and ultimately winning a teen video competition. She also covers the typical middle-school matters of friends, teachers, and boys. Tru is a talented pre-teen who has tough facts to face. A cure for Eddie is not very likely. She will grow up and he won't. Her diary is an honest look into what it's like to have a brother with special needs.

Subjects: mentally handicapped, middle school, physically handicapped, siblings, twins

173 Taylor, Theodore. *A Sailor Returns*. Blue Sky Press/Scholastic. 2001. Hardcover 160pp. Ages: 10 and up. ISBN: 0–439–24879–5 $16.95.

In the summer of 1914, in a small village on the coast of Virginia, eleven-year-old Evan Bryant's life is transformed by the visit of his long-lost sailor grandfather. Evan has a clubfoot and is small for his age. He can't run, and he wears a special shoe that is a "clumpish ugly thing." Kids make fun of him, calling him "big foot" or "shoe boy." He is embarrassed by his disability. Evan's grandfather, Tom "Chips" Pentreath, a fishing scalawag from Mousehole, England, was believed to be lost at sea in the late 1800s. When he arrives at Evan's home, grandfather and grandson bond immediately. They go fishing together and even build a rowboat. And the grandfather's sailing stories, which include references to distant, exotic islands and landforms, open a new world to Evan. Evan's grandfather, like Evan, is short and walks with a limp. When Evan remarks that they look funny walking beside each other, his grandfather responds that they'll walk proudly. He advises Evan to pay no attention to others. A murder occurs in the small village, and Evan's grandfather is a suspect. This leads to his confession to his family that he served time in prison for a murder committed in self-defense years ago. He leaves the village vindicated, but his visit has touched the lives of everyone there. This dramatic historical novel with its memorable characters provides insights into family bonds, honesty, and a boy's physical disability.

Subjects: boating, grandparents, historical fiction, intergenerational relationships, nature, physically handicapped, sports, Virginia

174 Taylor, Theodore. *Tuck Triumphant*. Doubleday. 1991. Hardcover 150pp. Ages: 9–12. ISBN: 0–385–41480–3 $14.95.

In the sequel to *The Trouble with Tuck* (Doubleday, 1984), fourteen-year-old Helen Ogden's blind Labrador, Friar Tuck Golden Boy, is led by Lady Daisy, a seeing-eye dog. Tuck's senses are sharp. He can "smell a passing dog a half-block away, hear leaves fall in the backyard." Tuck is challenged when the Ogdens adopt a six-year-old Korean orphan boy who is deaf and cannot speak. Tuck and Chok-Do bond right away. Helen thinks they sense each other's handicap. The Ogdens have a hard time with Chok-Do. They can't communicate with him and consider sending the boy back to the adoption agency. They repeatedly have him tested by doctors, and they explore other options of what to do with Chok-Do. Helen's father finally decides that the best thing for him would be to attend the California School for the Deaf in Riverside, three hours away. He could come home on weekends. Helen objects to this because Chok-Do would be less than "a part-time Ogden, not a real member of the family." Instead, she wants every-one to learn sign language and wonders if there is a way for Tuck, with his super-sensitive hearing, to serve as Chok-Do's "ears." Chok-Do is a curious boy. He wanders off and gets into serious trouble several times. And each time, Tuck and Daisy rescue him. Tuck's greatest challenge comes after his seeing-eye dog, Lady, is killed and Tuck uses all of his senses alone to save Chok-Do from a cougar and a raging mountain creek in a lightning storm. The near tragedy causes everyone to realize that Chok-Do belongs with them and not at the special school. Helen's mother, who is a teacher, decides to ask for a two-year leave of absence to stay home to teach Chok-Do. They will hire a sign language instructor and find a replacement guide dog for Tuck. The author acknowledges the California School for the Deaf and a teacher of the deaf for help with research for this novel.

Subjects: adoption, deaf, dogs—service, mutism, physically handi-capped, service dogs, sign language

175 Testa, Maria. *Thumbs Up Rico!* Albert Whitman & Co. 1994. Hard-cover 40pp. Ages: 5–10. ISBN: 0–8075–7906–8 $14.95. Illustrated by Diane Paterson.

Rico, who has Down syndrome, narrates three stories in this beginning chapter book. In the first story, " The First Time I Met Caesar," friendly Rico greets Caesar with "Hi, Buddy." Caesar responds by calling him "dummy." Rico is persistent. He wants Caesar for a friend and wants to play basketball with him. They do eventually become friends, and Caesar cheers Rico in his Special Olympics basketball game. In the second story, "Something for Nina," Rico is disappointed when his sister, Nina, is invited to a birthday party on the day of his big basketball playoff. Loyal Nina never misses his games. She can't decide what to do. Finally, Rico advises her to go to the party be-cause she needs time with her friends. In the third story, "Rico's Slam Dunk,"

Rico is discouraged in his art class at school. He can't seem to draw a picture that he is satisfied with. He asks everyone for ideas, but his drawings always look like mud. Then one day on the basketball court he gets his best idea, and that week he proudly displays his drawing of his own slam-dunk. Simple text reveals how Rico copes with challenges. Though Rico's age is never mentioned, the colorful watercolor paintings depict him as a middle grader.

Subjects: art, basketball, Down syndrome, elementary school, mentally handicapped, siblings, Special Olympics, sports

176 Thesman, Jean. *When the Road Ends*. Houghton Mifflin. 1992. Hardcover 184pp. Ages: 10 and up. ISBN: 0–395–59507–X $13.95.

Three foster children, narrator Mary Jack, rebellious fourteen-year-old Adam, and tiny Jane, who does not speak, leave the home of Father Matt Percy and his nervous wife to spend the summer with Aunt Cecile at her riverside cabin. Mary Jack is twelve years old and has lived with six different foster families that didn't want her for one reason or another. She is determined and sensible. She takes on responsibilities that no child should have to face. She desperately wants an "absolutely perfect family." Adam was abandoned by his mother. He is disenchanted and wears a constant scowl, but he proves to be loyal and resourceful in the end. Jane is seven or eight. No one knows for sure. No one knows her real name either. She was found beside the freeway with raw cuts across her back and burns on her neck. She had been whipped with a chain. She refuses to speak, hides under the bed, and sucks her thumb. She draws pictures but never includes herself in any of her drawings. When Father Matt's wife can no longer deal with the three "unbearable burdens," he sends them away with his sister Cecile. Cecile is recovering from a concussion she received in a car accident that killed her husband. Her left arm doesn't work quite right, and she suffers from aphasia. At the cabin, they struggle. The housekeeper runs off with the money, and mean, nosy campers cause trouble. Cecile's recovery is uneven, Adam disappears for a while, and Mary Jack is injured while chopping kindling. With the help of Al, a nice neighbor and old high school classmate of Cecile, they create a solution that will keep them from being split up and sent someplace worse. And fragile, little Jane warms up enough to reveal her name, Daisy, and begins to speak.

Subjects: adoption, elective mutism, physically handicapped

177 Thompson, Mary. *Andy and His Yellow Frisbee*. Woodbine House. 1996. Hardcover 24pp. Ages: 5–8. ISBN: 0–933149–83–2 $14.95. Illustrated by the author.

In describing her brother Andy, Rosie introduces young readers to autism. Andy likes to spin things, like coins, plates, and especially his yellow frisbee. Andy has a tough time talking and prefers to be in his own world. Sarah, a new girl at school, notices Andy and tries to befriend him by offering her pink frisbee to him. Rosie is afraid of how Andy might react but is heartened to discover that he doesn't need protection. Rosie and Sarah play frisbee, and Rosie hopes that maybe next time Andy will show Sarah how to spin a frisbee. Watercolor illustrations help convey the story's message of tolerance and acceptance. An author's note gives more information about children with autism.

Subjects: autism, elementary school, siblings

178   Thompson, Mary. *My Brother Matthew*. Woodbine House. 1992. Hardcover 28pp. Ages: 5–8. ISBN: 0-933149-47-6 $14.95. Illustrated by the author.

Matthew was born with a brain injury, and he moves and speaks differently from other children. He has trouble learning. His older brother, David, understands him better than anyone else in the story. Though David is often frustrated and resentful, the two boys experience much happiness playing space explorers, swimming, and going for walks. David reads books to Matthew and hopes that one day Matthew will be able to ride a bike. The story is told from David's perspective and compassionately portrays the range of emotions involved in having a special needs sibling. Watercolor illustrations bring to life the brothers' special bond.

Subjects: mentally handicapped, siblings

179   Todd, Pamela. *Pig and the Shrink*. Dell Yearling. 1999. Paperback 185pp. Ages: 9–12. ISBN: 0-440-41587-X $4.50.

Seventh grader Tucker Harrison needs a winning science fair project that will use science as a "tool for helping people" and that will get him into the State Math and Science Academy. He focuses on nutrition and obesity and uses Angelo "Pig" Pighetti as the subject of his experiment. Pig is the fattest kid in the seventh grade, weighing 180 pounds and standing just five feet four inches tall. His parents own and operate a pizza restaurant, and Pig is the "Michelangelo of spaghetti sauce." At first Pig is reluctant. He likes everything about food and doesn't want to lose weight because he likes himself the way he is. He even points out that some of the greatest people in history have been fat, like Winston Churchill and Santa Claus. But Tucker convinces Pig that he can teach him how to eat healthy foods and that by losing weight he will be helping himself as much as he is helping Tucker with his science fair project. Pig and Tucker have to deal with bullies who pick on Pig and the intriguing vegetarian and science fair competitor Beth Ellen. Beth Ellen questions Tucker's using Pig as a subject. She recognizes Pig's feelings and that he's a genius at the things that really matter. The experiment fails. The boys' friendship is threatened, and Pig actually gains weight. But in the end Tucker feels guilty about what he did to Pig and wants to withdraw his project from the competition. He concludes "that people have a right to decide for themselves who they are and what they want to be." The theme of acceptance is affirmed in Tucker's funny and wise first-person narration.

Subjects: middle school, overweight, self-perception

180   Tolan, Stephanie S. *Who's There?* Morrow Junior Books. 1994. Hardcover 235pp. Ages: 9–12. ISBN: 0–688–04611–8. Out of print.

After their parents are killed in a freak gas explosion, fourteen-year-old Drew and her eight-year-old brother, Evan, move to Rose Hill, their father's family home, to live with their long-lost Aunt Jocelyn and their ill grandfather. Evan has been mute for the eight months since their parents' deaths. He has not said a single word at school, with his friends, or even to Drew. At first Evan and Drew feel welcome. Evan gets no special attention, and Aunt Jocelyn treats him as if he is perfectly normal. They develop a crude but effective form of sign language. And Drew makes friends with a local boy, Will. They happily start to explore family history but soon discover that Rose Hill has mysteries. It is haunted by Amalie, the ghost of their evil and dangerous step-grandmother, and "Evan one," the ghost of their uncle who drowned when he was a young boy. In attempting to uncover the truth behind their father's break with the family and the deaths of his young brothers and stepmother, they rid Rose Hill of its ghosts, and Evan breaks through his grief-imposed silence. This contemporary ghost story is sufficiently spooky. An unexpected plot twist and the lack of psychological analysis of Evan's elective mutism make the novel entertaining.

Subjects: elective mutism, grief, mystery, siblings

181   Trembath, Don. *Lefty Carmichael Has a Fit.* Orca Book Publishers. 1999. Paperback 215pp. Ages: 12 and up. ISBN: 1–55143–166–1 $6.95.

Fifteen-year-old Lefty Carmichael is "the first right-handed person named Lefty in the world." When he is diagnosed with idiopathic epilepsy, his mother faints, his peers become hostile, and Penny, his girlfriend, is afraid to be alone with him. Lefty finds it difficult to return to his normal life after being hospitalized for a seizure. He has to deal with medication and overcome his fears, and he retreats into an overly cautious lifestyle. But life in his working-class neighborhood goes on. Lefty's mom and her tough girlfriends endlessly gossip and tell stories. His school friends party. His English teacher encourages Lefty's poetry writing. His oldest and best friend, Reuben, remains loyal. And a stronger Penny urges him to begin enjoying life again. Lefty realizes the importance of having people around at the best of times and the worst of times. He grows from a frightened kid into a self-sufficient young adult as others in his world increase their awareness of dealing with epilepsy. This is not so much a book about Lefty's condition as it is a look at how he and his family and friends react to his seizure disorder. Important information about dealing with seizures is integrated into the story.

Subjects: epilepsy, healthcare facilities, high school, seizure disorder

182 Trueman, Terry. *Stuck in Neutral.* Harper Collins. 2000. Hardcover 116pp. Ages: 12 and up. ISBN: 0–06–028519–2 $16.95.

This intense reading experience is about Shawn McDaniel, who has cerebral palsy. He cannot control any of his muscles. He cannot communicate at all and has been diagnosed as uneducable. No one knows he is sentient. He is a sane, intelligent teen with an incredible memory who is trapped in an uncontrollable body. He is witty and wise, a "secret genius," and happy to be alive. The entire story takes place inside Shawn's head. He spends his day in a wheelchair at a severely handicapped special day class or being cared for at home by his mother and older siblings. His father, an author and TV celebrity, left the family when Shawn was three years old because he was overwhelmed by Shawn's condition. His father loves him deeply and has written a Pulitzer Prize–winning poem about being a parent of a child with cerebral palsy. He is tormented by Shawn's disability, fascinated with euthanasia, and increasingly comments about ending his son's pain. Shawn suspects that his father is considering killing him in order to end his perceived suffering. Both father and son desperately want to understand each other, but they cannot. The story goes beyond the voice of a helpless teen trapped in a broken body and an attempt to help others see through the eyes of the disabled. It is the story of a father who is torn apart by what he doesn't know and can't control. Readers must draw their own conclusions as

Shawn's father's quandary is left unresolved. What makes this eye-opening book even more compelling is the fact that the author is the father of a son with cerebral palsy much like Shawn, who is diagnosed as being profoundly developmentally disabled. In the book, he creates a character based on what life might be like for a person like Shawn or his son. But no one really knows.

Subjects: cerebral palsy, physically handicapped, special education, wheelchairs

183 Tuitel, Johnnie, and Sharon Lamson. *Discovery on Blackbird Island* (Gun Lake Adventure series Book 3). Cedar Tree Publishing. 2000. Paperback 108pp. Ages: 8–12. ISBN: 0-9658075-2-5 $5.99.

In Book 3 of the Gun Lake Adventure series, Johnnie Jacobson and his friends discover a puppy and a kitten on isolated Blackbird Island in Michigan. They solve the mystery of who's abandoning the animals and why. Their sleuthing leads to the arrest of a man for cruelty to animals and illegally delivering the pets to a company that does research on animals. What sets this engaging, action-filled mystery series apart is Johnnie, who has cerebral palsy. He uses a wheelchair and rides a handcycle. Nothing stops him. He does everything his detective friends do, only differently. The author, Johnnie Tuitel, has cerebral palsy, and a portion of the proceeds from the sale of the series goes to support a nonprofit organization that provides wheelchairs for people who could not otherwise obtain such equipment. Other titles in the series for middle-grade readers are *The Barn at Gun Lake* (1998) and *Mystery Explosion* (1999).

Subjects: cerebral palsy, physically handicapped, wheelchairs

184 Turk, Ruth. *The Doll on the Top Shelf*. Owl's House Press. 1998. Hardcover 32pp. Ages: 4–8. ISBN: 1-891-992-0213 $21.95. Illustrated by Per Volquartz.

This beautiful and tenderhearted book is for visually impaired and sighted children. Every page is written in both Braille and type. It's the Christmas season, and Annie May is a very plain doll that is moved by Mr. Carenot, the toyshop owner, to the top shelf to make room for the pretty, sparkly dolls and toys that will sell. On Christmas Eve a lady and her granddaughter, Natalie, come into the shop looking for a doll on sale. Because Natalie is blind, she chooses a doll based not on appearance but by how it feels. Natalie chooses Annie May, and it becomes the best Christmas for both of them. The book is richly illustrated in oils, scratchboard etching, and computer-generated art. An author's note provides information about Louis Braille and reading and writing the Braille alphabet.

Subjects: blind, Braille, grandparents, intergenerational relationships, physically handicapped, visually handicapped

185   Walters, Eric. *Rebound.* Stoddart Kids. 2001. Hardcover 262pp. Ages: 10 and up. ISBN: 0–7737–3303–5 $15.95.

In seventh grade Sean McGregory used to skip classes, not complete his homework, talk back to teachers, and get into fights. This year he wants a fresh start. He can't get into trouble or he won't be on the eighth-grade basketball team. David Ross was in an accident, is now paralyzed from the waist down, and is bitter and angry about being confined to a wheelchair. He has just moved to Sean's school, and Sean has been assigned to be his host. At first neither boy is happy about this. David appears to be confident, strong, and brave. He doesn't want anyone's help. He fights his own battles. Sean feels he doesn't share David's characteristics. It's not that he's a coward. It's just that he's not like David. However, both boys do have tempers. As they grow from each other's strengths and weaknesses, so does their friendship. They play basketball, have girlfriends, write an A+ report on nerve regeneration, and manage to stay out of trouble. Sean learns a great deal about David's wheelchair world when he uses David's spare wheelchair and accompanies him through town. He experiences how difficult or easy it is to physically get around and also how society reacts to people in wheelchairs. Much detailed, factual information is given about using a wheelchair and the challenges a person in a chair faces. Things take on a different perspective for both boys. They discover "it isn't what you do with the shots you make, but the ones that don't go in. The rebounds." The author, who is a teacher, social worker, and family therapist, used a wheelchair to accompany the co-founder of LINK around his hometown, just like Sean and David did. Thus, he accurately portrays "what the abilities of individuals with disabilities are, and . . . how society reacts to people with disabilities." He points out that "the greatest disability is attitude." The LINK Foundation creates awareness and opportunities to include the disabled in sports, fitness, and recreation. Contact phone numbers are provided.

Subjects: basketball, middle school, physically handicapped, sports, wheelchairs

186 Wanous, Suzanne. *Sara's Secret.* Carolrhoda Books, Inc. 1995. Hardcover 40pp. Ages: 5–8. ISBN: 0–87614–856–9. Out of print. Illustrated by Shelly O. Haus.

Sara's secret is her five-year-old brother, Justin, who was born with cerebral palsy and is severely mentally retarded. At her new school she doesn't want her classmates to know about Justin. She doesn't want them to be cruel to him or call him retarded, as they did at her old school. There "nobody understood that even though my brother can't walk or talk or feed himself, or even sit up, he can still make me happy." Sara's teacher announces that they will be talking about disabilities in class, and as an assignment they should think of one thing that would help a person with disabilities. It would be even better if they could bring something to class. Sara doesn't know what to do. When her parents learn about the assignment, her mom says that Sara should have a lot to say and that she could almost teach the class. Her dad writes a note to Justin's teacher giving permission for Sara to bring Justin to her class. Her guilt and embarrassment prevent her from concentrating in school. Keeping Justin a secret isn't easy. She decides that Justin is her brother, not a secret, and brings him to her class. She introduces him and explains about cerebral palsy and mental retardation. Her classmates ask many questions, which she and her teacher answer. Sara faces up to her feelings, honestly and sincerely. Soft watercolors, mostly in shades of orange, help tell an important story that validates the feelings of children who have siblings with disabilities. An author's note offers possible causes for cerebral palsy and mental retardation and explains that the effects of both disabilities can be mild or severe.

Subjects: cerebral palsy, elementary school, mentally handicapped, siblings

187 Welch, Sheila Kelly. *Don't Call Me Marda.* Our Child Press. 1990. Paperback 138pp. Ages: 9–12. ISBN: 0–9611872–4–7 $12.95.

Written from eleven-year-old Marsha O'Dell's point of view, this thought-provoking novel explores Marsha's emotions and reactions to her parents' decision to adopt a developmentally delayed child. Marsha believes it is a mistake. Eight-year-old Wendy arrives and disrupts the household. She acts younger than she is and has a lot of spunk. She moves into Marsha's bedroom, destroys and loses some of Marsha's Barbie dolls, and steals the affection of Marsha's cat. At school, Marsha's classmates make obnoxious comments about Marsha and her retarded sister. And Wendy can't even pronounce Marsha's name correctly. Marsha lists in her diary ten terrible things that Wendy has done, ranging from eating all the best cereals to not liking Butterscotch, Marsha's pony. Wendy is even worse than Marsha imagined. After months, Marsha finally breaks down and tells her parents how Wendy has changed her life and made her feel so alone and helpless. Marsha's parents appreciate her honesty and want her input. Because of this, Marsha begins to feel better. At school, she is invited to help in the special education classroom because she is so good in English, and she starts to give pony-riding lessons to kids in the neighborhood. The story concludes positively. It's Marsha's twelfth birthday, and Wendy presents the cake she so creatively decorated and sings "happy birthday, dear MARSHA." The author, who is a teacher of developmentally delayed students and the mother of adopted special needs children, realistically portrays Marsha's learning to love and appreciate her adopted sister.

Subjects: adoption, elementary school, mentally handicapped, special education

188 Whelan, Gloria. *Forgive the River, Forgive the Sky*. Eerdmans Books. 1999. Paperback. 111pp. Ages: 9–12. ISBN: 0–8028–5158–X $6.00.

Twelve-year-old Lily Star is angry at the Sandy River. She can't forgive it because last year her father died while fishing on the river. She and her mother leave their cabin in the woods and move to an apartment over the hardware store in town following the sale of the cabin to T. R. Tracy. T. R. is a former test pilot who is now confined to a wheelchair. Much like Lily, he can't forgive the sky because of a plane crash that took from him the use of his legs. He moved to the country to get away from people who only saw his wheelchair and to prove that he doesn't need anyone. T. R. builds a fence around the land Lily knows and loves, but it doesn't keep her from the great blue herons, beaver lodges, and rosy pink moccasin flowers she treasures. Strong-willed Lily ignores T. R.'s attempts to drive her away. She befriends him, and by the end of the story they both forgive nature and accept their situations. T. R. even returns to the sky to test planes designed for disabled pilots. The descriptions of the Michigan flora and fauna are true to life and poetic in this thought-provoking short novel.

Subjects: grief, Michigan, nature, physically handicapped, wheelchairs

189 Whelan, Gloria. *Hannah*. Random House. 1991. Paperback 60pp. Ages: 8–12. ISBN: 0–679–82698–X $3.99. Illustrated by Leslie Bowman.

In 1887 Michigan, nine-year-old Hannah doesn't go to school because she is blind. She is also limited by the ignorance of the time and her parents' over-protectiveness. Hannah tells of Miss Robbin, the new teacher, who comes to board with her family and persuades them to allow her to attend school. Miss Robbin appreciates Hannah's creativity and is determined to help Hannah become self-sufficient. The scene where Miss Robbin takes Hannah on a tour of her farm is especially sensitive. School is not easy at first, but eventually Hannah proves that she can learn by listening and using Braille books. Black and white pencil drawings add a sense of time and place to this brief historical novel for intermediate readers.

Subjects: blind, Braille, elementary school, historical fiction, physically handicapped, teachers

190 White, Ruth. *Belle Prater's Boy*. Yearling (Bantam Doubleday Dell). 2001. Paperback 196pp. Ages: 9–12. ISBN: 0–440–41372–9 $5.50.

Set in Appalachia in the 1950s, this book's message is that it is only what's in the heart that counts. When twelve-year-old Gypsy Arbutus Leemaster's cross-eyed, hill country cousin, Woodrow, moves next door to live with his grandparents, Gypsy thinks she'll learn about the family mystery: the disappearance of Woodrow's mother, Belle Prater. Woodrow doesn't talk much about his mother, but as they spend time together the cousins become close friends. Woodrow is a fascinating character. He is thoughtful and brilliant. He tells witty stories and can be a bit mischievous. He is teased about his thick glasses and being cross-eyed. Kids ask him if he can look two directions at once. He confides in Gypsy that what he really wants is for his eyes to be straight, so they'd look just like hers. Gypsy is the town beauty. She has long blond hair and worries that people don't see the real Gypsy under all that golden hair. Everyone cares more about her looks than she does. She asks, "What does it matter how pretty or ugly a person is?" and "Why do folks even notice Woodrow's eyes?" because he's such a good person. Old Blind Benny is another important character in this moving story. Blind Benny, even with his sightless eyes, can see with perfect clarity because he can see beyond appearances. The cause of Woodrow's sadness is revealed, and he eventually tells the truth about his mother. Gypsy, too, has secrets and can't get over her father's death. Both characters are transformed as they solve the family mystery and accept their past tragedies.

Subjects: Appalachia, blind, grief, historical fiction, mystery, self-perception, visually handicapped

191   White, Ruth. *Memories of Summer.* Farrar, Straus & Giroux. 2000. Hardcover 135pp. Ages: 9–12. ISBN: 0–374–34945–2 $16.00.

It is 1955, and thirteen-year-old Lyric, sixteen-year-old Summer, and their father move from rural Virginia to Flint, Michigan, where automobile assembly line jobs are available. Attractive Summer has always taken care of Lyric, but after their move Summer drastically changes. She won't go to school, lets her appearance deteriorate, and speaks gibberish. The diagnosis is schizophrenia. Lyric and her father struggle to take care of Summer but are forced to institutionalize her when she becomes dangerous. Summer's descent into mental illness brings on bewilderment, anger, and embarrassment in Lyric; but as she understands her sister's illness, she grows into a strong young woman. The characters are vividly drawn through Lyric's honest first-person narration and dialogue that will evoke both laughter and tears.

Subjects: emotional problems, healthcare facilities, mentally ill, schizophrenia, siblings

192   Willis, Jeanne. *Susan Laughs.* Henry Holt. 1999. Hardcover 36pp. Ages: 4–8. ISBN: 0–8050–6501–6 $15.00. Illustrated by Tony Ross.

Rhyming couplets describe Susan's moods and activities. Susan laughs, sings, flies, and swings. She is good, bad, happy, and sad. She dances and swims. She plays with her friends, works hard in school, and listens to her father read bedtime stories. Not until the end of the book is it revealed that Susan uses a wheelchair. The short and sweet text emphasizes what she can do. Despite her physical challenges, this plucky little girl is "just like me, just like you." Children will identify with Susan's elfish appearance and mischief-loving manner. The colorful pencil and crayon drawings are lively and playful. Both Susan's expressions and those of her cat will make young readers laugh.

Subjects: elementary school, physically handicapped, wheelchairs

193   Wittlinger, Ellen. *Razzle.* Simon & Schuster. 2001. Hardcover 247pp. Ages: 12 and up. ISBN: 0–689–83565–5 $17.00.

Geeky, fifteen-year-old Kenyon Baker tells the story of the summer before his junior year in high school. He and his older retired parents have just moved to Truro, on Cape Cod, from Boston to renovate and run a beachfront resort. Ken paints the cottages and supervises plumbing repairs in return for his own cottage, where he can set up a photographic darkroom. Ken is tall and skinny. He is sensitive, confused, and sometimes sarcastic. There is never a place where he fits in, unless it's his darkroom. But that doesn't count because there, he's alone. The first person Ken meets is eccentric Razzle Penney. She is named for Raziel, the Angel of Mysteries. She is the "neatnik junkmeister" who works at the Swap Shop at the town dump. Razzle is "downright strange" and "much too outspoken for a young girl." She, like Ken, is lonely. She explains that she can never live anywhere but Truro because the rest of the world is full of Perwims. Perwims are people without imaginations. At first Razzle accuses Ken of being a Perwim. But meeting Razzle is a turning point in Ken's life. She helps him adjust to his new surroundings, and they develop a close friendship. Ken's photography is inspired by Razzle, his muse. He takes a striking series of photos of Razzle, which he intends to exhibit at the Dump Dance and Art Show. Everything is fine until Ken meets beautiful Harley. Harley has been Razzle's enemy since third grade. She is boy-crazy, and Ken falls for her. She manipulates him into taking photos of her and showing them alongside the photos of Razzle at the art show. Consequently Ken's relationship with Razzle falters. She is deeply hurt. At the same time Razzle's alcoholic mother returns to town and confesses the truth about Razzle's father. Ken and Razzle do not pick up the pieces of their friendship. But Ken, because of knowing "the craziest girl on Cape Cod," has learned a lot about loyalty and tolerance. Other offbeat characters in this lively, thought-inspiring novel are Billie, Razzle's hippie grandmother who owns twelve dogs; Lydia, an old artist who is a cottage guest and loves the smell of the ocean; and Frank, a gay plumber who is hired to repair the cottages.

Subjects: art, grandparents, high school, intergenerational relationships, popularity, self-perception

194 Wood, June Rae. *About Face*. G. P. Putnam's Sons. 1999. Hardcover 265pp. Ages: 9–12. ISBN: 0–399–23419–5 $19.99.

An intense three-day friendship allows two dissatisfied, yet very different, thirteen-year-old girls to see that "happiness is not having what you want, but wanting what you have." Glory Bea Goode hates living in a junk shop–rooming house in Turnback, Missouri, with her Gram. Glory has a port-wine birthmark that reaches from her left ear almost to her nose. Gram calls it a beauty mark. Glory calls it ugly. Since kindergarten, kids "backed away from her in fear," and she "backed away from them in shyness, in pain, in shame at being different." She still puts up with stares, whispers, insults, and the nickname Clot Face. Glory desperately wants a friend and hopes she's found one in Marvalene Zulig. Marvalene lives in a tiny trailer that's part of a touring carnival. She fries and sells corn dogs in her father's stand. Her mother used to be a dancer before she had a stroke, but now she is Madame Zulig, psychic reader and fortuneteller. Marvalene would give anything to live in a big old house instead of either selling to the public or moving to the next town, seven days a week. She, too, desperately wants a friend. Marvalene charms Glory with her psychic powers, but really she has just peeked at Glory's diary. They get involved in a mystery surrounding a secretive boarder. And they work through carnie/townie prejudices. The girls end up going their separate ways, but they both learn to believe in themselves. Marvalene discovers that wherever the carnival goes, that's where she wants to be. And Glory realizes that if she thinks of herself as imperfect, other people will too, and if she stops dwelling on her imperfection, she will project a better image.

Subjects: birthmarks, facial disfiguration, grandparents, intergenerational relationships, Missouri, self-perception

195 Wood, June Rae. *The Man Who Loved Clowns*. Hyperion Paperbacks. 1995. Paperback 224pp. Ages: 12 and up. ISBN: 0–7868–1084–X $4.95.

Patterned after the author's brother, thirty-five-year-old Punky is Delrita's uncle, who lives with her family in a small town in Missouri. Punky, who has Down syndrome, has the mind of a little boy and is always happy-go-lucky. He loves clowns, his Jellybean lunch box filled with crayons, and singing into a pretend microphone. An only child, Delrita is devoted to Punky with all her heart, yet she is also ashamed of him. She watches after him and protects him from the outside world. She doesn't want friends who will make fun of Punky. She doesn't want to be noticed and is happy being invisible to her eighth-grade classmates. When Delrita's parents are killed in a traffic accident, she and Punky must live with her aunt and uncle. This forces Delrita to discover that she needs friends and that other people can learn to love Punky and be proud of him. Delrita's aunt and uncle send him to a workshop where he is taught to use his capabilities and be freed by what he can do, instead of being restricted by what he can't do. The book supplies an education about people with disabilities and how things have changed for people like Punky. This is a realistic and vivid portrait of the challenges that face a child growing up with a disabled family member. It is involving and enriched with touches of humor.

Subjects: Down syndrome, mentally handicapped, middle school, Missouri

196 Wood, June Rae. *When Pigs Fly.* Penguin Putnam. 1995. Paperback 259pp. Ages: 8–12. ISBN: 0–698–11570–8 $5.99.

Thirteen-year-old Buddy Rae has a nine-year-old sister, Reenie, who has Down syndrome. Reenie spends most of her day in a special education class and is mainstreamed for art and music. Loyal Buddy protects Reenie when she is stared at, ridiculed, and tormented because she is different. Other things complicate Buddy's life as well. Her best friend, Jiniwin, is angry about her parents' divorce, starts drinking, and even accuses Reenie of stealing her purse. Because Buddy's father is unemployed, her family has to sell their home and move to a dilapidated old farmhouse on the outskirts of town. Buddy has to ride the bus with strange Dallas Benge, care for her hard-boiled-egg baby as a Family Living class project, and battle blacksnakes in her backyard. She believes things will get better "when pigs fly." But her warm, caring family supports her, and things do start to look up. Buddy is a devoted sister to Reenie, who is a magical character with a gentle, loving heart and soul. This inspiring story shows what it's like to live with a Down syndrome sibling and teaches that it's not important what other people think of you, but what you think of yourself.

Subjects: Down syndrome, mentally handicapped, middle school, siblings, special education

197 Wright, Betty Ren. *Out of the Dark.* Scholastic. 1995. Hardcover 128pp. Ages: 9–12. ISBN: 0–590–43598–1 $13.95.

Twelve-year-old Jessie and her parents have recently moved into her grandmother's house in the country while her grandmother is away. Jessie's mother is unhappy with her job, and her father is having difficulty writing a book on his experiences in Vietnam. Jessie's new friend Toni is disabled, but her disability is never explained clearly. She wears a misshapen shoe with an inch-thick sole. She is bitter and thinks that she doesn't have many friends because of her foot. However, she can ride a bike and run, and her disability doesn't play a role in the story. It's really a ghost story. Jessie is having chilling nightmares about the old abandoned schoolhouse and a blond woman who seems to want to harm Jessie. Her grandmother's girlhood diaries offer clues to the identity of the ghost. When Jessie and Toni are trapped in the old schoolhouse vault, Jessie fears that the ghost will be her end. But when Jessie's grandmother returns to town, Jessie finds out who the ghost really is and why she is haunting her. This horror novel about a ghost who is seeking revenge will please young mystery fans.

Subjects: grandparents, intergenerational relationships, mystery, physically handicapped

198 Yamanaka, Lois-Ann. *Name Me Nobody*. Hyperion Paperbacks. 2000. Paperback 229pp. Ages: 12 and up. ISBN: 0–7868–1466–7 $5.99.

Fourteen-year-old Emi-Lou Kaya lives with her grandmother and attends intermediate school on Hawaii's Big Island. Her mother left when Emi-Lou was three years old, and she doesn't know who her father is. She is overweight and the popular Japanese girls call her Emi-oink and Emi-fat. She feels like a nobody because she is ashamed of her size and doesn't fit in with even the nerds, geeks, or zeroes. Her best friend is Yvonne Vierra. She pulls Emi-Lou into her world of softball and volleyball and shoplifts diet pills for her. She puts Emi-Lou on a strict weight loss plan, which is successful. But Emi-Lou's new, thin body confuses her. It used to be that she was unpopular, poor at sports, and without a boyfriend because she was fat. Now she's not fat and still doesn't know where she fits in. Emi-Lou also has another worry. Yvonne is spending too much time with Babes, a friend from the softball team, and rumors fly that they are "butchie." Emi-Lou wants Yvonne to be "normal" and is angry about losing her best friend. However, she does begin to feel happier about herself as two members of the high school volleyball team become interested in her. Sterling is a handsome athletic star who is nice to her. Kyle charms her into writing stories for him and later attempts to rape her. Gradually, with the help of her grandmother, Emi-Lou realizes that she can't change Yvonne and that she shouldn't judge her. Emi-Lou is a complex teen who journeys into self-knowledge and confidence. She tells her story in Hawaiian Creole English.

Subjects: baseball, grandparents, Hawaii, high school, intergenerational relationships, middle school, overweight, sports, volleyball

199 Yang, Dori Jones. *The Secret Voice of Gina Zhang*. American Girl, Pleasant Company Publications. 2000. Hardcover 215pp. Ages: 9–12. ISBN: 1–58485–204–6 $12.95.

As twelve-year-old Chinese immigrant Gina Zhang enters her new school in Seattle, her voice disappears. She feels very out of place and her throat tightens up. But she can speak at home, and her mama reassures her that it's just first-day-of-school tension. Then it gets worse. She wants to speak, but she can't. Everyone watches her and thinks she is dumb. She hopes her teacher will see behind the silence and know she is a normal person. Only Priscilla, who is overly chatty and friendless, knows that Gina can understand English words. As weeks go by Gina practices English at home, but the minute she enters the school door the words get trapped in her throat. Everyone's patience and understanding wear thin as they expect Gina to act like a normal student. Still, Priscilla is her only friend, "like a precious gem." Gina is placed in a special needs class, but that makes her feel stupid, humiliated, and even more out of place. Being quite imaginative, Gina retreats into a private fantasy world complete with yarn people she creates. Priscilla discovers Gina's fantasy and her storytelling gift, but Gina is afraid to let anyone else know her secret. Priscilla finally convinces Gina to share her inner story in a written form. When the book ends, Gina still does not speak at school, but she writes messages on the board. She knows she can be "smart and brave and nice." Her teachers and classmates see that she has a brain despite her silent exterior. A touching scene occurs earlier in the book when Gina's father, who had ordered her to speak at school, reveals that when he was a boy in China during the Cultural Revolution, he did not speak. For ten years he was silent because of a terrible incident that happened in first grade. He doesn't know why, but it became easier for him to speak when he reached age sixteen. The doctors say that many children who stop speaking have a mother or a father who had the same problem as a child. Gina's father knows it will be different for her in America today, where doctors and teachers understand the problem and can treat it. The author, who spent ten years in Asia, writes an important story about the challenges facing students learning a new language and culture and the message that silent does not mean stupid.

Subjects: Asians, elective mutism, elementary school, special education

200   Zimmett, Debbie. *Eddie Enough*. Woodbine House. 2001. Hardcover 44pp. Ages: 5–10. ISBN: 1–890627–25–9 $14.95. Illustrated by Charlotte Murray Fremaux.

Eddie Minetti is a third grader who always gets in trouble at school. He forgets his lunch, is late, is accused of cheating, knocks things off his teacher's desk, and slams doors when he gets angry. He moves too fast, talks too much and too fast, and even listens too fast. His out-of-control behavior earns him the nickname "Eddie Enough" because his teacher has "had enough, Eddie, enough!" Tests reveal that Eddie has attention-deficit hyperactivity disorder. His teacher, principal, therapist, and parents help and support him. And medicine helps him look before he leaps. He learns to slow down, make better choices, and feel better about himself. He becomes

"Eddie Just Right." An author's note explains ADHD in simple terms. Black and white drawings from unusual perspectives depict Eddie's active movements and honest emotions. The author is a therapist for special needs students.

Subjects: attention-deficit hyperactivity disorder, elementary school, learning disabled.

Title Index

Titles appear in alphabetical sequence, followed by author and Annotated Bibliography entry number.

Author Index

Authors appear in alphabetical sequence, followed by title and Annotated Bibliography entry number.

Age-level Index

Age-levels appear, followed by author and title in alphabetical sequence with the Annotated Bibliography entry number.

Subject Index

Subjects appear in alphabetical sequence, followed by title of book and Annotated Bibliography entry number.

About the Author

MARILYN WARD is Associate Professor of Education at Carthage College, where she teaches Children's Literature, Creative Arts, and Social Studies Methods. She coordinates the children's library and directs a program for gifted and talented students. She was a contributor to *Outstanding Books for Young People with Disabilities* (International Board on Books for Young People, 1999).

Printed in the United States
72353LV00003B/235